THE WINES
IN THE
SUPER MARKETS
2016

NED HALLEY

foulsham
LONDON • NEW YORK • TORONTO • SYDNEY

W. Foulsham & Co. Ltd
for Foulsham Publishing Ltd
The Old Barrel Store, Drayman's Lane, Marlow, Bucks SL7 2FF

Foulsham books can be found in all good bookshops and direct from
www.foulsham.com

ISBN: 978-0-572-04546-3

Text copyright © 2015 Ned Halley
Series, format and layout design © Foulsham Publishing Ltd

Cover photographs © Thinkstock

A CIP record for this book is available from the British Library

The moral right of the author has been asserted

Typeset in the UK by Chris Brewer Origination
Printed and bound in Great Britain by Martins the Printers Ltd

Contents

Why do we do it?	5
A sense of place	11
Spot the grape variety	15
Looking for a branded wine?	19
Pick of the year	21
Aldi	25
Asda	31
The Co-operative	45
Lidl	53
Majestic	59
Marks & Spencer	71
Morrisons	83
Sainsbury's	95
Tesco	109
Waitrose	129
Making the most of it	147
Wine and food	153
What wine words mean	156
Index	189

—Why do we do it?—

Shopping for wine in a supermarket is like climbing Everest. Why do you do it? Because it's there. This is how the supermarkets have moved in so successfully on the wine business. They figured out long ago that if shoppers were coming in for bread, meat and vegetables, why expect them to go anywhere else for wine? Back in the early days, of course, when wine was an occasional luxury, a handful of cheap brands would be sufficient to meet demand.

Now, it's another story. Every supermarket is awash. They've got 80 per cent of the take-home ('off-licence') component of an overall market now worth £10 billion a year. Six out of ten British adults count themselves as wine drinkers. You can see why the supermarkets take it all so seriously.

Don't listen to smooth-talking merchants in striped shirts who say supermarket wine is all mass-produced bilge made to a price for drinkers who don't know any better. I have visited enough supermarket-supplying winemakers – including châteaux in Bordeaux – to know that a lot of skill and dedication goes into producing even the humblest retailer's own-label vintages. And when the budget's tight, the skill and dedication are that much more to be admired.

At the production end, it's a tough business, very competitive. Around the world demand for wine is flat, or falling. In the wine-producing nations of Europe, domestic thirsts are drying up dramatically. Leading producer by volume, Italy, reports that home sales of 104 litres per head in 1975 have plummeted to 29 litres in 2015. In the UK, by some measures the world's biggest wine importer, consumption of all alcoholic drinks, wine included, is in gradual decline. But the capacity for wine production worldwide is expanding enormously.

Where will it all lead? While we await the shake-out, I suggest relaxing with a glass of really good, sensibly-priced wine to contemplate the possibilities. For the moment, there is a glut of good wine, and the supermarkets have cornered a significant share of it. And thus, this book.

The premise is that you're already in the supermarket. My mission is not to urge you there. It's to put you in the picture once you're in the wine aisle. You've got the other groceries. Might as well look at the wine. But there are hundreds of them. The shelves are plastered with promotional talkers. Your eye is lured this way and that by familiar, much-advertised brands, by drastic discounts, by half-recognised names you believe you might remember from previous expeditions. How to choose?

My task, after tasting as many supermarket wines from current vintages as I possibly can, is to make suggestions. It's down first to quality, then to value. I'm happy to recommend the cheapest wines – after all, nine out of every ten bottles we buy to drink at home are priced under £6 – and taste these as a matter of priority. But mid-price wines – let's define those at between £6 and £10 – tend for obvious reasons to be more interesting. They account for the great majority of the wines described in this book.

Whether your taste is in big reds or light reds, rich whites or dry whites, or any other styles, I aim to highlight the best buys in the supermarket of your choice. As the retailers tend to arrange their wines first by colour, then by nation of origin, I follow the same logic in my listings. Price is next. I list the wines in ascending order.

Price counts for a lot, and I faithfully append to every wine mentioned in the book the price I was quoted by the retailer. But there's an inevitable caveat. Prices change all the time. In the past, the gyrations in the value of sterling against the euro have played havoc with wine prices. But the Pound now has a fairly well-established exchange rate against the troubled continental currency. I hesitate to be specific here in print but the recent 1.40 rate is a major improvement on the sub-1.20 value that prevailed before 2015. This will have made euro-trading a lot more certain (and profitable) for the supermarkets, so along with low inflation, there's reason to hope for price stability. Sterling's value against other overseas currencies is less predictable, I suppose, but given the economic vagaries affecting major supplying nations such as Argentina and Chile, South Africa and even Australia, the Pound starts to look quite respectable. Even the Government made an effort in 2015, bringing in the first Budget in living memory to leave the excise duty on wine exactly where it was. At £2.05 on a 75cl bottle of still wine it is still scandalous, of course.

To return to the point, prices for wine do fluctuate, but in the present state of the market it's quite likely to be downwards. This will be thanks largely, of course, to the promotions that supermarkets perpetually apply to every kind of merchandise, wine included.

Given the supermarket shake-ups in which even Tesco has seemed to wobble on its very foundations, price wars will surely continue. And I wonder too if the progressive monopolisation of wine by supermarkets will be reversed by the famous trend away from the big weekly shop to the quick dash. Traditional wine merchants could be the beneficiaries if they can compete.

For the moment, I suspect discounting will continue to be the supermarkets' primary weapon, in wine as in everything else. No doubt the phoney deals will persist, where the retailer displays a silly price for the legally prescribed period then halves it for the illusory effect. But there are real deals too. These are particularly attractive when applied to the retailers' own-label wines. They're the wines the supermarkets are most proud of. Morrisons say that 90 per cent of all the wines carrying their own brand are made under their own control. Maybe it's true of all of the supermarkets. They're staking their reputations on these products. So they are not going to slap fake standard prices on them in order to facilitate the occasional promotional blitz.

Own-label ranges comprise the majority of wines I recommend here. Their diversity increases every year, their quality is consistent and most are of convincing value. And yet all the supermarkets regularly discount their own-label wines. It's where the real bargains are.

And on top of individual price cuts, we can now look forward to regular blanket promotions. It's usually 25 per cent off all wines for a period of a week or so. Wines on individual offer might well be doubly reduced. So frequent are these promotions that you might wonder if any of the supermarkets sell any wine at all between times.

A sense of place

This book categorises the wines by nation of origin. It is largely to follow the manner in which retailers arrange their wines, but also because it is the country or region of origin that still most distinguishes one style of wine from another. True, wines are now commonly labelled most prominently with their constituent grape variety, but to classify all the world's wines into the small number of principal grape varieties would make for categories of an unwieldy size.

Chardonnay, Sauvignon Blanc and Pinot Grigio are overwhelmingly dominant among whites, and four grapes – Cabernet Sauvignon, Grenache, Merlot and Syrah (also called Shiraz) – account for a high proportion of red wines made worldwide.

But each area of production still – in spite of creeping globalisation – puts its own mark on its wines. Chardonnays from France remain (for the moment at least) quite distinct from those of Australia. Cabernet Sauvignon grown in a cool climate such as that of Bordeaux is a very different wine from Cabernet cultivated in the cauldron of the Barossa.

Of course there are 'styles' that winemakers worldwide seek to follow. Yellow, oaky Chardonnays of the type pioneered in South Australia are now made in South Africa, too – and in new, high-tech wineries in New Zealand and Chile, Spain and Italy. But the variety is still wide. Even though the 'upfront' high-alcohol wines of the New World have grabbed so much of the market, France continues to make the elegant wines it has always made in its classic regions. Germany still produces racy, delicate Rieslings, and the distinctive zones of Italy, Portugal and Spain make ever more characterful wines from indigenous grapes, as opposed to imported global varieties.

Among less expensive wines, the theme is, admittedly, very much a varietal one. The main selling point for most 'everyday' wines is the grape of origin rather than the country of origin. It makes sense, because the characteristics of various grape varieties do a great deal to identify taste. A bottle of white wine labelled 'Chardonnay' can reasonably be counted on to deliver that distinctive peachy or pineappley smell and soft, unctuous apple flavours. A Sauvignon Blanc should evoke gooseberries, green fruit and grassy freshness. And so on.

For all the domination of Chardonnay and Cabernet, there are plenty of other grape varieties making their presence felt. Argentina, for example, has revived the fortunes of several French and Italian varieties that had become near-extinct at home. And the grape that (in my view) can make the most exciting of white wines, the Riesling, is now doing great things in the southern hemisphere as well as at home in Germany.

Among the current market trends, the rise of rosé continues apace. Now accounting for one out of every eight bottles of still wine sold, the choice of pink brands has simply exploded. I have certainly found a greater number of interesting pinks than might have been imagined a few years ago, but there are still plenty of dull ones with suspiciously high levels of residual sugar, so choose carefully.

Rosé wines are supposed to be made from black-skinned grapes. After the crush, the skins are left in contact with the juice for long enough to impart a pleasing colour, and maybe some flavour with it, and the liquids and solids are then separated before the winemaking process continues as it would for white wine.

Some rosés are made merely by blending red and white wines together. Oddly enough, this is how all (bar one or two) pink champagnes are made, as permitted under the local appellation rules. But under prevailing regulations in Europe, the practice is otherwise forbidden. Elsewhere in the world, where winemaking is very much less strictly standardised, blending is no doubt common enough.

It is, I know, a perpetual source of anguish to winemakers in tightly regulated European nations that they have to compete in important markets like Britain with producers in Australia, the Americas and South Africa who can make and label their wines just as they please. Vineyard irrigation, the use of oak chips, and the blending in of wines from other continents are all permitted in the New World and eschewed in the Old.

But would we have it any other way? No winemaker I have met in Bordeaux or Barolo, Bernkastel or Rias Baixas seriously wants to abandon the methods and conventions that make their products unique – even with an eye on creating a global brand. And in this present difficult economic climate for wine drinkers (and winemakers) worldwide, this assurance of enduring diversity is a comfort indeed.

Spot the grape
variety

The character of most wines is defined largely by the grape variety, and it is a source of innocent pleasure to be able to identify which variety it is without peeking at the label. Here are some of the characteristics to look for in wines from the most widely planted varieties.

White

Chardonnay: Colour from pale to straw gold. Aroma can evoke peach, pineapple, sweet apple. Flavours of sweet apple, with creaminess or toffee from oak contact.

Fiano: Italian variety said to have been cultivated from ancient Roman times in the Campania region of southern Italy. Now widely planted on the mainland and in Sicily, it makes dry but soft wines of colours ranging from pale to pure gold with aromas of honey, orchard fruit, almonds and candied apricot. Well-made examples have beautifully balanced nutty-fresh flavours. Fiano is becoming fashionable.

Pinot Grigio: In its home territory of north-east Italy, it makes wines of pale colour, and pale flavour too. What makes the wine so popular might well be its natural low acidity. Better wines are more aromatic, even smoky, and pleasingly weighty in the manner of the Pinot Gris made in Alsace – now being convincingly imitated in both Argentina and New Zealand.

Riesling: In German wines, pale colour, sharp-apple aroma, racy fruit whether dry or sweet. Faint spritz common in young wines. Petrolly hint in older wines. Australian and New Zealand Rieslings have more colour and weight, and often a minerally, limey twang.

Sauvignon Blanc: In the dry wines, pale colour with suggestions of green. Aromas of asparagus, gooseberries, nettles, seagrass. Green, grassy fruit.

Semillon: Colour can be rich yellow. Aromas of tropical fruit including pineapple and banana. Even in dry wines, hints of honey amid fresh, fruit-salad flavours.

Viognier: Intense pale-gold colour. Aroma evokes apricots, blanched almonds and fruit blossom. Flavours include candied fruits. Finish often low in acidity.

Red

Cabernet Sauvignon: Dense colour, purple in youth. Strong aroma of blackcurrants and cedar wood ('cigar box'). Flavour concentrated, often edged with tannin so it grips the mouth.

Gamay: One of the most distinctive grapes of France, where it is the exclusive variety in the red wines of Beaujolais. Colour can be purple, with a suggestion of blue; nose evokes new-squashed raspberries, and there may be a hint of pear drops, an effect of carbonic maceration, a vinification technique used in Beaujolais. Fruit flavours are notably summery, juicy and refreshing.

Grenache: Best known in the Côtes du Rhône, it tends to make red wines pale in colour but forceful in flavour with a wild, hedgerow-fruit style and hints of pepper.

Malbec: Originally a Bordeaux variety, Malbec has become principally renowned in Argentina, where it thrives in the high-altitude vineyards of Mendoza. Wines are characterised by very dark, dense colour, and by aromas that perhaps fancifully evoke leather and liquorice as well as dark fruits. Flavours include black fruits with chocolate and spice; the wines are often grippy with retained tannin.

Merlot: Dark, rich colour. Aroma of sweet black cherry. Plummy, rich, mellow fruit can be akin to Cabernet but with less tannin. May be hints of bitter chocolate.

Pinot Noir: Colour distinctly pale, browning with age. Aromas of strawberry and raspberry. Light-bodied wine with soft-fruit flavours but dry, clean finish.

Sangiovese: The grape of Chianti and now of several other Italian regions, too. Colour is fine ruby, and may be relatively light; a plummy or even pruny smell is typical, and flavours can evoke blackcurrant, raspberry and nectarine. Tannin lingers, so the wine will have a dry, nutskin-like finish.

Shiraz or Syrah: Intense, near-black colour. Aroma of ripe fruit, sometimes spicy. Robust, rich flavours, commonly with high alcohol, but with soft tannins. The Shiraz of Australia is typically much more substantial than the Syrah of the south of France.

Tempranillo: Colour can be pale, as in Rioja. Blackcurrant aroma, often accompanied by vanilla from oak ageing. Tobacco, even leather, evoked in flavours.

There is more about all these varieties, and many others, in 'What wine words mean' starting on page 156.

Looking for a branded ───── *wine?* ─────

While the supermarkets' own-label wines – the likes of the Sainsbury's Taste the Difference and the Tesco Finest ranges – are obviously exclusive to the respective chains, branded wines are very often stocked by any number of different retailers.

If you're looking for a favourite brand, do check the index to this book on page 189. If I have tasted the wine and given it a mention, it is most likely to appear under the heading of the supermarket that hosted the tasting. But you might be accustomed to seeing this particular wine in another chain altogether.

I cannot give space in a pocket-sized book to repetitions of notes on popular brands that might very well be sold by each of the supermarket chains. But I do try to keep tasting the bestselling brands in hope of finding something positive to say about them.

Pick of the year

On the unreliable basis of analysing the 30 maximum scores I have recorded this year, Tesco comes out as top wine retailer with 6, closely pursued by Marks & Spencer and Sainsbury's, both with 5. Asda comes next with 4, Waitrose and Morrisons with 3 and the Co-op 2. Aldi and Majestic have 1 apiece.

If I were to chart my pick of the supermarkets on a wider evaluation of their wine performances, this is not the order I would put them in. But ranking these giant retailers is an invidious undertaking at best.

More interesting is the national distribution of my top scores. Out of the 30, France has taken 13. No other country comes close. Spain follows with 4, Italy and South Africa with 3 each and Germany and Chile get 2. Australia, Portugal and Uruguay are singletons. Where is Argentina? New Zealand? Sounds odd, I'll admit.

My plea is that I don't pick out wines because I like the countries they come from. No offence intended to France here, of course. Nor do I prefer wines that come from particular supermarkets. Well, I try not to.

Red wines

Morrisons Côtes du Rhone	Morrisons	£4.75
Wine Atlas Frapatto 2014	Asda	£4.97
Estevez Cabernet Sauvignon Carmenère Reserva 2011	Aldi	£4.99
Waitrose Mellow and Fruity Spanish Red 2014	Waitrose	£4.99
Good Ordinary Claret 2014	Waitros	£5.19
Finest Fitou Domaine D'Aubermesnil 2013	Tesco	£5.99
Toscana Rosso 2012	M&S	£6.00
Tesco Finest Côtes Catalanes Grenache 2014	Tesco	£6.99
Domaine du Colombier Chinon 2012	Sainsbury's	£7.00
Noster Nobilis Priorat 2013	Asda	£7.98
Pisano Cisplatino Tannat 2014	M&S	£9.00
Extra Special El Meson Rioja Gran Reserva 2005	Asda	£9.97
Graham Beck Antony's Yard 2013	Majestic	£9.99
Palataia Pinot Noir 2013	M&S	£10.00
Taste the Difference Barbaresco 2012	Sainsbury's	£10.00
Valdivieso Single Vineyard Cabernet Franc 2010	Morrisons	£13.99

White wines

Simply Chenin Blanc	Tesco	£4.49
Tesco Anjou Blanc 2014	Tesco	£4.99
Hen Pecked Picpoul de Pinet 2014	Waitrose	£7.99
Tapada de Villar Vinho Verde 2014	M&S	£8.00
Mineralstein Riesling 2014	M&S	£10.00
Rully Domaine Marguerite Dupasquier 2013	Asda	£10.50
Thelema Sutherland Chardonnay 2012	Co-op	£10.99
Taste the Difference Pouilly Fumé 2014	Sainsbury's	£12.00
M Signature Chablis Premier Cru 2012	Morrisons	£14.99
McGuigan The Shortlist Chardonnay 2011	Tesco	£15.00

Sparkling wines

Les Pionniers Champagne Brut	Co-op	£16.99
Sainsbury's Champagne Blanc de Noirs Brut	Sainsbury's	£20.00
Finest Grand Cru Vintage Champagne Brut 2007	Tesco	£24.99

Fortified wine

A Blend of Amontillado Medium Dry
Sherry   Sainsbury's   £5.50

Aldi

 During 2015 Aldi overtook Waitrose in the supermarket stakes. The German discounter is now in sixth place in terms of market share, behind the Big Four and the Co-op. If Aldi continues to grow at its present rate – and why would it not – it will ease past the Co-op some time during 2016.

This astonishing progress is not all down to Aldi's wine offering. While many of its product lines are unquestionably competitive, very few of the wines are. I have tasted a good number from the range, including some kindly sent to me by Aldi after they neglected to ask me to their 2015 press wine tasting (was it something I said last year?) and have found some very sound buys.

Aldi has a mid-price own-label range under the cumbersome 'Exquisite Collection' brand, and most of the other wines are exclusive. You won't find them anywhere else. They do special wines in high seasons such as Christmas, but all those I have featured here are from the core range, so you should be able to find them in your local branch year-round.

What Aldi does not have is shelves burgeoning with overpriced global-brand wines, as other supermarkets do. Good for Aldi in this respect.

As to the price-quality ratio that is the mantra of this guide, Aldi does not yet compare significantly with its giant rivals – Waitrose included. But I am well aware that in future this might change.

RED WINES

ARGENTINA

 8 Exquisite Collection Uco Valley
Malbec 2012 £5.99

Rather refined variation on the usually strapping Andean Malbec theme, this is dark and deep with notions of violet and even liquorice amid the ripe blackberry soup; 14% alcohol.

AUSTRALIA

7 Bushland Estate Shiraz 2012 £4.59

Jammy everyday Shiraz for the more robust taste at a very low price; 14% alcohol.

 8 Exquisite Collection Limestone Coast
Cabernet Sauvignon 2013 £6.49

Cushiony-plump but clearly outlined ultra-ripe blackcurrant fruit in this textbook value-for-money varietal; 14% alcohol.

CHILE

 8 Andara Merlot 2013 £3.99

Middleweight black-cherry wholesome party red at a genuine bargain price.

10 Estevez Cabernet Sauvignon Carmenère
Reserva 2011 £4.99

Robust, intense and blackcurrant-rich this is nonetheless poised, wholesome and balanced – no sign of overripeness or jamminess. Best value Chilean of the year. If this has been succeeded by a new vintage, do take a punt.

 8 Estevez Pinot Noir 2013 £4.99

Slinky ripe sour-cherry Pinot of substance.

RED WINES

FRANCE

♟ 9 **Pinot Noir Vignobles Roussellet** £4.39
Warm, black-cherry Pinot of dense colour (for Pinot),
remarkable togetherness of fruit and sturdiness of weight;
made by Loire Valley producer Lacheteau: how do they
do it at this price?

NEW ZEALAND

♟ 9 **Exquisite Collection Wairarapa
Pinot Noir 2013** £6.99
This needs a little time in the glass to lose the boiled-
sweet smell that can first confound the senses. Thereafter,
a delectably juicy, raspberry-ripe classically poised Kiwi
Pinot of terrific charm; strong crimson colour; well-knit
fruit and finishing pure and brisk.

SPAIN

♟ 8 **Toro Loco Tempranillo 2014** £3.79
I can barely believe the price of this 'superior' Utiel-
Requena wine. It's rustic but not rough with bright purple
fruit and a healthy balance.

PINK WINES

SPAIN

♟ 8 **Toro Loco Rosé 2013** £3.69
The cheapest rosé of the year and by no means the least
of them, this Utiel-Requena wine has a near-fluorescent
magenta colour, a bracing raspberry and lemon nose, a
crisp attack of pink fruit and lively acidity; it's bold, dry
and unflinching. Not many pink wines you can say this
sort of stuff about; 11.5% alcohol.

WHITE WINES

**9 Exquisite Collection Clare Valley
Riesling 2013** £6.99
Assertive limey dry wine in the Aussie manner (a different animal from the Mosel model) this is outstanding, expressing racy, appley Riesling character; 11.5% alcohol. If Aldi could source their wines at this level across the range, they would conquer the world.

9 Vignobles Roussellet Sauvignon Blanc £4.69
Full, ripe 'vin de France' from the Loire is bursting with green fruit, gooseberry juiciness and general joyfulness; textbook Sauvignon at an off-the-page price.

8 Chardonnay Vin de Pays d'Oc 2014 £4.99
Safe, fresh stone-fruit and coconut sunny Chardonnay at a safe price.

7 The Exquisite Collection Gavi 2014 £5.49
Zingy with a fair bit of residual sweetness, a friendly, orchard-fruit example of the popular Piedmont dry white.

8 Freeman's Bay Pinot Gris 2014 £5.69
Apricot in colour and (perhaps, admittedly, by synaesthetic association) the nose of this fruit-salad wine tells you at once it's in the style of Alsace rather than the dull Italian Pinot Grigio rendition. It's a bit soft but has a quirky grapefruit acidity. Worth a try, especially at the price.

8 Freeman's Bay Sauvignon Blanc 2014 £5.89
Plenty of sunny-ripe gooseberry-peapod fruit in this perky Marlborough wine at a keen price.

WHITE WINES

9 Exquisite Collection Marlborough Sauvignon Blanc 2014 £7.99

Good one, expansive with gooseberry and grassy aromas, nettly-bright and crisp but with artful rich residual sweetness in crafty balance; a convincing Kiwi Sauvignon at a persuasive price.

SPARKLING WINES

9 Philippe Michel Crémant de Jura 2012 £7.29

Another convincing vintage for this annual bargain from France's mountainous border country east of Burgundy, softly foaming in the crémant ('creaming') manner and apple-fresh with all-Chardonnay fruit; soft, easy-drinking at a very keen price.

9 Champagne Veuve Monsigny Brut £11.99

At the price – a pound down on last year's – this shows some class with its tiny-bubble mousse, bakery smell and lush, crisp but creamy rush of flavour.

9 Prosecco Valdobbiadene Superiore Extra Dry £7.49

After tasting scores of Proseccos over the years I can find none I like better than this, regardless of price. It's very pale, vigorously frothy and redolent of elderflower with crisp-pear fruitiness and a nifty acidity; 11% alcohol, and, as advertised, extra dry.

SPARKLING WINES

 **7** **Freeman's Bay Marlborough**
Sparkling Wine £9.99
Unmistakably Sauvignon Blanc and definitely sparkling,
this turns out exactly as you might expect. Slaves to the
gooseberry glories of the sweeter kind of Sauvignon
should try it.

Asda

Asda is the sleeping giant of the supermarket-wine world. While its rivals seem forever to be hyping their ranges in television commercials, noisily slashing prices and congratulating themselves on winning endless medals in tasting competitions, Asda gets quietly on with building a marvellous range of wines, many of them own-label, of real quality and diversity, and at standard prices that put even the German discounters firmly in the shade.

It's all perception of course. Isn't everything? Maybe it's just mine that confounds my forays to Asda's wine aisles: I find them the least clearly arranged of any of the big retailers, and am often unable to find particular wines I have come in for. How do casual browsers find anything, I wonder.

It's worth adding, though, that shoppers attracted by good label designs will notice a welcome new arrival at Asda. The Wine Atlas range is a geographically delineated collection of wines from across the world with attractively illustrated, topographically themed labels. I have included ten wines from the range, all under £7, in this year's entry. They are good.

Fifteen of the wines featured here cost £5 or under. It is easily the best range I have found anywhere below this price threshold. And bear in mind that Asda, along with all the others, is perpetually reducing wine prices in seasonal promotions.

This year I tested Asda's dedicated online service The Wine Shop by ordering a mixed case. It was simple to work the website (it has to be, for me) and delivery was both prompt and free.

RED WINES

9 Trivento Reserve Malbec 2013 £7.99
Mass-market brand maybe, but this muscular Mendoza pure varietal is uncommonly distinctive in its dark, intense, violet-veiled perfumes and savours. Oak-matured and substantial (14% alcohol) it has a firm but yielding tannic grip, and looks likely to round out for several years yet. Top buy. I did also try a 187ml bottle – good, but not for keeping.

9 Zilzie Shiraz Viognier 2013 £4.85
Blockbuster blend is sinewy and spicy with the darkest black-fruit relish and oak-contact smoothness. Viognier adds 'femininity' to Shiraz an Aussie winemaker once told me, and maybe that's the secret of this one. The ludicrously low price helps a bit, too; 14% alcohol.

8 Zilzie Merlot 2012 £4.85
Healthy black-cherry nose and bags of perky balanced matching fruit in this easy charmer at what seems a strangely low price; I could find no fault and fancy it would make a nice red with a fish pie; 14% alcohol.

**9 De Bortoli Family Reserve
Cabernet Sauvignon 2013** £6.75
Irresistibly clingy and long-flavoured blend with one-eighth Merlot is as vigorous as it is rich and in fine balance; made for roast lamb, it tastes well above price.

8 Extra Special Yarra Valley Pinot Noir 2013 £7.98
Big plump Pinot in the Aussie manner by excellent De Bortoli winery is backed up with a bit of Shiraz; long, ripe and relishable.

RED WINES

8 **Mayu Sangiovese 2012** £5.37
Sangiovese is the grape of Chianti, but this is a different animal, with ripe but pleasingly abrasive briar fruit finishing nutskin dry; 14% alcohol.

9 **Cono Sur Bicicleta Pinot Noir 2014** £7.49
This very likeable wine from Concha y Toro's Cono Sur is reportedly 'The UK's No. 1 Pinot Noir'. If it really is, it deserves to be – a seductively coloured and perfumed slinky cherry-summer-soft-fruit insinuator of warmth and balance, earthy in the inimitable Pinot manner, and full of juicy plumptiousness. I reopened a bottle a day after and I promise it had become even more friendly and silky. Also sold at the other three supermarket giants.

8 **Errazuriz Estate Merlot 2013** £8.98
Elegantly defined plummy Merlot of uplifting purity.

9 **Casillero Reserva Privada 2013** £9.98
Concha y Toro flagship blend of Cabernet Sauvignon with a little Syrah looks good and lives up to it: satisfying succulent cassis formula in ideal balance; a safe bet and a charming wine.

8 **Extra Special Shiraz 2013** £5.00
Grrr – I wish they wouldn't use the Australian affectation Shiraz for what is the Syrah grape at home in France. That apart, this dark, ripe and spicy vin de pays d'Oc is deliciously well-knit and satisfying at what seems a needlessly low price; 14% alcohol.

CHILE

FRANCE

RED WINES

8 Wine Atlas Côtes de Roussillon 2014   £5.47
Untypically light in weight for Roussillon, but you get plenty of peppery, garrigue-scented blackberry and plum fruit.

8 Extra Special Côtes du Rhône Villages 2012 £6.75
Proper limpid peppery hill-herb and warm-briar Côtes du Rhône of middle weight and forceful presence.

8 La Côterie Vacqueyras 2013   £7.97
Keenly priced for a wine from this prestige Rhône appellation, it's well-knit, juicy and spicy; 14% alcohol.

8 Extra Special Bordeaux Supérieur
Château Roberperots 2012   £10.00
Not just any old claret ('Bordeaux Supérieur' is an all-too generic designation) this has a promising dense colour, cedary-cassis nose and sleek, unified, distinctly claret-like fruit. Nice oak, convincing quality wine.

9 Château de La Dauphine 2011   £11.00
This nice package from the Fronsac appellation of Bordeaux is nine parts Merlot to one Cabernet Franc, making a sleek and darkly juicy cassis claret with firm but friendly tannin. Wine Shop online only.

9 Mercurey Béjot 2012   £11.50
Lovely silky Pinot Noir from the Chalonnais, Burgundy's least-trumpeted outpost, with heart-warming strawberry scent, well-defined soft-summer-fruit ripeness and creamy texture en route to a bright, tight finish.

FRANCE

RED WINES

FRANCE

🍷 8 Extra Special Châteauneuf du Pape 2014   £13.50
In my day, Châteauneuf du Pape was always special, but
now everybody does it – at a price. This one is worth a
mention because in spite of its callow youth (the best of
these wines take years to come round) it's already warmly
integrated and savoury with toasty-ripe Mediterranean
black fruits and does taste something like Châteauneuf.

ITALY

🍷 10 Wine Atlas Frapatto 2014   £4.97
From new brightly labelled Asda range, a delightfully
ripe and sunny island (Sicily) red with a holiday savour
of warm spicy wild brambly fruits with a convincing
fullness. It's a marvel at the price, from an elusive grape
that sometimes produces slightly sweet wines, but here
is perfectly balanced and finished. I even like the label's
Byzantine Sicilian scenery. One to seek out.

🍷 8 Wine Atlas Marzemino 2013   £5.97
Cheery (and cheerily labelled) picnic red from sub-Alpine
Trentino; purple and bouncy but firm with briary fruit.

🍷 9 Extra Special Primitivo 2011   £7.00
This dark, tarry but friendly Puglia roast-meat red has
long savoury black fruit with a pleasing bitter-chocolate
centre to the flavour; lipsmacking.

🍷 8 Extra Special Chianti Riserva 2011   £7.98
Intense and sinewy proper Chianti-style cherry and
hedgerow fruit with the right kind of dry nutskin finish;
it's been aged two years in oak casks but the fruit is still
to the fore.

RED WINES

🍷 8 Extra Special Barbera d'Asti 2012   £8.00
Juicy, brambly and spicy middleweight made smooth by long oak maturation and heady with 14.5% alcohol.

🍷 9 Squinzano Orbitali Riserva 2011   £8.98
I am incapable of resisting the name Squinzano. It's a little town in Puglia with a DOC for red wines mainly from Negroamaro grapes. This one is suitably black-ruby in colour with juicy blackberry fruit in wholesome ripeness with a lick of toffee richness. Wine Shop online only.

🍷 9 Extra Special Barolo 2010   £15.00
All Barolo ought be extra special, but isn't. I like this one, though, for its alluring limpid ruby colour going orange at the rim and the enticing coffee-cherry, almost spirity nose followed up by slinky oaked bitter-cherry, grippy proper Nebbiolo (constituent grape) fruit. Lovely stuff by Piedmont giant Araldica.

🍷 8 Amarone della Valpolicella Cantine Riondo 2011   £16.00
Speciality Verona wine now almost commonplace; dense, dark and toasty with the right amarone ('bitter') edge to the rich, plump, plummy near raisiny fruit; 14.5% alcohol.

🍷 8 Marlborough Sun Pinot Noir 2013   £6.75
Kiwi Pinot is expensive and this makes a nice intro. Pale but healthy, quivering with cherry charm and raspberry juiciness, crisp and clean. Ignore the gimmicky newsprint label.

🍷 8 Extra Special New Zealand Pinot Noir 2013 £8.48
Sleek Marlborough wine has enticing aroma and balance at a fair price.

RED WINES

Asda (vertical, left margin)

PORTUGAL

🍷 9 Extra Special Dão 2013 £5.00

Made largely from Port grapes, this is a handsomely presented bargain with gripping blackberry character and hints of clove and raisin made slinky by oak contact.

🍷 8 Extra Special Douro 2013 £5.00

Like the ES Dão above, a wine made from Port grapes but this time grown in Port country. It does hint at the intensity and darkness of the fortified wine, with good grip.

🍷 8 Wine Atlas Fetasca Neagra 2014 £4.97

Bright in colour with redcurranty fruit, a skilfully made distinctive summer red from a native grape variety.

SPAIN

🍷 8 Extra Special Old Vines Garnacha 2013 £5.00

Distinctive sappy, spicy Cariñena cheapie something like a Ribera del Duero with dark minty savour made sleek with a bit of oak contact; 14% alcohol.

🍷 8 Wine Atlas Cigales Tempranillo 2011 £5.97

Artful contrivance in the Rioja style. Plump cassis charm and a clear vanilla note; 14% alcohol.

🍷 9 Casa Luis Reserva 2011 £6.98

Rollickingly ripe redcurrant and bramble juice bomb in perky harmony finishing very clean and dry, made in Cariñena region from Tempranillo and Garnacha (the Rioja formula) and aged a year in oak for an extra richness.

🍷 8 Gran Bajoz Toro 2011 £6.98

Big, sweetly ripe but firmly gripping, black-fruit winter warmer; 14% alcohol. Definitely a sausage red.

RED WINES

SPAIN

🍷 **10 Noster Nobilis Priorat 2013**   £7.98

Somebody must be buying this perennial prodigy because the vintage keeps updating. This one has a lavish expensive perfume of ripest thick-skinned plum, blackcurrant and spice and flavours that live entirely up to it all with added gaminess and truffle. It's dense, already developed (even if reds from the revered Priorat region are supposed to live for decades), slinky and gorgeous; 14.5% alcohol. I have been following this wine from the 2007 vintage – priced back in the day at £9.98 – and it's as good as ever, even so young. Stock up.

🍷 **10 Extra Special El Meson Rioja Gran Reserva
      2005**   £9.97

It's vulgar I know, but this gets an unconditional 10 score because it's ridiculously cheap as well as ridiculously delectable. Colour's gently browning, as you might expect at 12 years old, but it's alive with lush strawberry ripeness by no means sidelined by the creamy vanilla from oak contact. Perfect old-fashioned reassuring Rioja. Yum.

WHITE WINES

AUSTRALIA

🍷 **8 McGuigan The Shortlist Chardonnay 2012 £13.97**

The product, I am told, of an exceptionally sunless and wet vintage in the Adelaide Hills, this does have a cool-climate (or Burgundian, one might say) style and peaches-and-cream richness married to elegant, cool minerality; really outstanding.

CHILE

🍷 **8 Extra Special Chilean Sauvignon Blanc 2013 £5.98**

Leyda Valley pure varietal; has an asparagus pong and brisk green fruit.

WHITE WINES

Asda

CHILE

 **8 LFE Selección de Familia Sauvignon Blanc
2014**   **£7.98**
Same producer, Luis Felipe Edwards, as the ES Sauvignon above but with big peapod and asparagus whiff and exuberant tropical lushness amid the grassy rush; a nice match for shellfish.

FRANCE

 9 Wine Atlas Côtes de Thau 2014   **£4.97**
From new 'Wine Atlas' brand at Asda, a breezy item from the Mediterranean coast with grapefruit freshness but without the sourness and a controlled sweetness. It looks commercial but tastes better than that. Sauvignon is the main grape, but not the main thrust in the flavour.

8 Extra Special Chardonnay 2014   **£5.00**
Substantial gold-coloured ripe-apple Pays d'Oc of easy charm at a good price.

8 Extra Special Viognier 2014   **£5.00**
With its apricot character and curious oiliness, Viognier can be an acquired taste. This one, from the Languedoc, is notably bright and dry.

9 Wine Atlas Marsanne 2014   **£5.47**
Rebranded for the colourfully presented Wine Atlas range, this is a new spin on the former 'Asda Marsanne' about which I have been raving for years. Made as before by commendable Foncalieu, it artfully combines tropical aromas and flavours with perky freshness and a citrus twang.

WHITE WINES

**8 Château Salmonière Muscadet de Sèvre
et Maine Sur Lie 2014** £6.50
Generous and twangy brassica and sea-grassy classic
leesy mussel-matcher from the bracing vineyards at the
Atlantic mouth of the Loire.

8 Wine Atlas Touraine Sauvignon Blanc 2014 £6.75
Taste this Loire Valley zinger 'blind' and you might well
mistake it for a New Zealand wine. A deliberate effect?
Likeable green, grassy Sauvignon by any light.

**9 Extra Special Bordeaux Blanc
Château Roberperots 2014** £7.00
Instantly likeable pure Sauvignon has a vivid tang,
savoury-green freshness and almost-piercing acidity,
leavened with a lick of oak contact. Asda's Master of
Wine Phillippa Carr hazards the notion that this 'could
be the "new" Marlborough Sauvignon Blanc because of
its tasty umami character': you heard it here first.

8 Le Grand Clauzy Sauvignon Blanc 2014 £7.45
Not sure of the provenance – 'from 20-year-old vineyards
on the Atlantic coast', says Asda – but no doubt of the
crisp, authentic Sauvignon character in the bone-dry,
amazingly tangy citrus-edged grassy fruit. Stands out a
mile; 11.5% alcohol.

8 Extra Special White Burgundy 2013 £9.00
From Chardonnay grapes sourced both in the Côte d'Or
and the Mâconnais, this richly coloured burgundy strikes
an intriguing balance between lush creaminess and apple-
crisp fruit.

WHITE WINES

**🍷 10 Rully Domaine Marguerite Dupasquier
2013** £10.50
Rully is a relatively obscure AC of Burgundy's Chalonnais where they make some fabulous dry Chardonnay. This is one of them: luscious but stone-pure, jumping with sweet peach and apple-pie fruits, creamy from oak contact but daisy-fresh. A real treat but only in 149 bigger stores.

**🍷 8 Extra Special Chablis Domaine de la Levée
2013** £11.00
Nice gunflint minerality in this plush golden Chardonnay by Chablis celebrity Jean-Marc Brocard; decent value for this quality.

🍷 9 Dr L Riesling 2014 £7.49
Cracking new vintage of this iconic moselle pops with apple perfumes and delivers a rush of racy-grapy fruit in sublime balance; a mood-lifting aperitif with just 8.5% alcohol.

🍷 8 H Prinz von Hessen Rheingau Riesling 2012 £8.97
This regal hock in zesty style is quite dry with apple freshness, a lick of honeyed ripeness and a citrus edge; 11% alcohol.

🍷 8 Wine Atlas Grillo 2014 £4.97
Aromatic dry Sicilian aperitif; has a surprising muscat-grapy element in the fruit. I liked it.

🍷 8 Extra Special Soave Classico 2014 £6.98
Austere at first sip, this offers a satisfying balance between green fruit and almondy richness with a precise lemon acidity. Good Soave; 11.5% alcohol.

WHITE WINES

ITALY

🍷 **8** **Extra Special Pinot Grigio 2014** £8.00
Decent Trentino wine by giant Cavit is aromatic, dry, even edgy, with a smoky pungency and long white fruit. Good example at the price.

🍷 **8** **Aupouri Sauvignon Blanc 2014** £5.75
Clear asparagus nose on this beguiling Marlborough wine, matching grassiness with a cautious sweetness which might be down to the spoonful of Chardonnay mysteriously added to the mix. Jolly cheap.

NEW ZEALAND

🍷 **9** **Extra Special Marlborough Sauvignon Blanc 2014** £6.00
Brisk and efficient wine with a nice nettly vigour and long green flavours, really quite ritzy, especially at this price. It includes 1% Gewürztraminer, it says here. Is this some sort of joke?

🍷 **8** **Kiwi Cove Sauvignon Blanc 2014** £7.98
Is the name a tilt at France's Kiwi Cuvée Sauvignon Blanc? This is a much better wine, bristling with gooseberry and seagrass lushness, surging fruit and tangy acidity.

S. AFRICA

🍷 **8** **Wine Atlas Feteasca Regala 2014** £4.97
Aromatic but dry-finishing party wine from indigenous Romanian grape variety; has a crafty trace of sweetness amid the orchardy-peachy fruit.

SPAIN

🍷 **9** **Extra Special Fairtrade Chenin Blanc 2014** £7.00
Much to allure here: lemon-gold colour, nectar-bearing bloom and crisp orchard fruit on the nose and long, healthy fresh green-tinged ripe white fruit flavours finishing tight and citrus tangy. Fairtrade and more than fair value too. What's not to like?

WHITE WINES

9 **Extra Special Palacio de Vivero Rueda 2014** £5.00
I shouldn't go back over old ground, but I commended
the 2013 vintage of this wine at £8.00. Now it's £5.00
and the 2014 is full with ripe vegetal-grassy Verdejo fruit
and stimulating citrus acidity. A natch match for smoked
mackerel.

SPAIN

8 **Alba Signature Albariño 2013** £6.00
Breezy Rias Baixas dry wine with trademark peaches-
and-brassica fruit and a seaside twang of freshness.

8 **Albariño Albanta 2013** £12.00
Luxury spin on the rightly popular seaside wine of
Galicia's rias Baixas, this is intense, almost resiny, in
its aromatic greengage-stone-fruit sheen with lush long
flavours and lemon edge. Wine Shop online only.

SPARKLING WINES

FRANCE

8 **Extra Special Louis Bernard Premier Cru
Champagne** £19.95
Lively biscuity house non-vintage champagne is on
reliably good form.

ITALY

7 **Filippo Sansovino Millesimato Prosecco
Brut Magnum** £18.00
Bumper double-size bottle adds pizzazz to this perry-like
frother's rather sweet pear fruit.

SPAIN

8 **Casa Luis Cava Rosado** £5.00
Magenta busily sparkling wild-strawberry-fruit party
fizz looks a bit of a fright but is quite fun and almost
irresistibly cheap; 11.5% alcohol.

The Co-operative

Get this. Last year, 27 million bottles of the wine sold in the Co-op was bulk-shipped. It came in tanks, not glass, and was bottled here. This policy, says Simon Cairns, drinks boss at the Co-op, 'saved 4,222 tonnes of carbon dioxide emissions – the equivalent to the electricity needs of 18,759 households for a year'.

I love it. Drink wine. Save the planet. There's quite a lot of this sort of thing at the Co-op, what with Fairtrade – 'we are proud to be the UK's largest retailer of Fairtrade wines' says Simon – and the recent naming of the Co-op as the UK's 'Ethical Drinks Retailer of the Year'. They won this award last year, too.

There is much to like on the wine shelves of the Co-op. Own-label wines, including the 'Truly Irresistible' range, account for a growing proportion, and offer the best value (no doubt UK bottling helps keep the prices down), but there are plenty of fine branded wines, including the stupendous Thelema Chardonnay from South Africa that gets a top score this year.

You will not find rarities like this in your local Co-op convenience store, sadly. But given the total of outlets has now passed 4,000 nationwide – two new Co-ops open every week – you are probably not far from a store with a really good selection.

RED WINES

8 **The Co-operative Argentine Malbec 2014**   **£4.99**
'The perfect partner with steak or spicy sausages' proclaims the exuberant label, a new poster-style design lately adopted for the Co-op's own basic range. Good sturdy varietal that lives up to the billing.

9 **The Co-operative Fairtrade Merlot 2014**   **£6.99**
This new addition to the Co-op's formidable Fairtrade range is an absolute whopper: the darkest cherry-and-bitter-chocolate depths of flavour in a smooth but convincing balance.

9 **The Co-operative Fairtrade Truly Irresistible Malbec 2013**   **£8.49**
The brandings are getting a bit entangled, but this is still the Co-op's perennial straightforward delicious varietal with leather-and-spice aromas, dark chocolate richness to the ripe mulberry fruit and all-round winter-warming appeal.

8 **The Interlude Pinot Noir 2014**   **£6.49**
In spite of the soppy, pretentious labelling, I very much liked this white pepper-scented, dry, raspberry-ripe contrivance. A fleeting but memorable red to drink cool.

8 **Ferngrove Cabernet Sauvignon 2012**   **£10.99**
Darkly minty monster from Frankland River in South Australia is immediately likeable for its generous ripeness and piquancy; 14% alcohol.

9 **Montes Reserva Cabernet Sauvignon 2013** **£7.99**
I was suddenly seized with a liking for this familiar brand's opaque colour and profound Bordeaux-style elegance. Creamily rounded, mature-tasting cassis-cigar-box plumminess, all at such a fair price.

RED WINES

CHILE

🍷 **8** **The Co-operative Truly Irresistible Pinot Noir 2013** £7.99
Pale but convincing Casablanca: cheery-nosed, raspberry-ripe part-oaked Pinot – crisp but lingering; 14% alcohol.

FRANCE

🍷 **8** **Les Crouzes Old Vines Carignan 2014** £6.49
Grippy, ripe and spicy Languedoc from the Carignan, a grape usually blended for colour and tannin with nobler names but here darkly savoury and enhanced by contact with 'French oak staves' in the tank.

🍷 **9** **Les Jamelles Réserve Mourvèdre 2012** £7.49
Seek out this unusual Mediterranean varietal for its long, dark briar fruitiness and pungent garrigue highlights; the 2013 vintage, not tasted, should nevertheless be just as good.

🍷 **7** **Pécharmant Clos Montalbanie 2010** £7.99
Decanted for the tasting, this smart package from the Dordogne was still a bit tough, but showing good prospects of big briar-blackcurrant fruit from its Merlot-Cabernets mix. A forward investment at a very reasonable price, worth a punt; 14% alcohol.

🍷 **9** **Château Jouanin 2012** £9.49
From Castillon, the easternmost outpost of Bordeaux, an intensely coloured and chewily constructed Merlot-based, part-oaked black-fruit claret with years ahead of it but already plumply satisfying. Castillon, scene of England's final defeat of the 100 Years War in 1453, is unfashionable, but this wine inspires détente.

RED WINES

FRANCE

Y 9 The Co-operative Truly Irresistible
Domaine de La Noblaie Chinon 2013 £9.99
Redcurrants wrapped in vine-leaves are irresistibly
evoked in this juicy, brisk and eager Cabernet Franc red
from the historic Loire town and appellation of Chinon.
Distinctively delicious and even better served gently
chilled.

Y 9 Château Fonréaud 2008 £11.99
This posh bottle from the Bordeaux commune of Listrac
is showing agreeable age-related tan-ruby colour and
sweet cassis glow on the nose; a complete, supple and
silky claret at a fair price.

ITALY

Y 8 The Co-operative Barbera 2013 £4.79
This purple, brambly, perky Piedmont spaghetti red is
both wholesome and cheap.

Y 8 The Co-operative Truly Irresistible
Montepulciano d'Abruzzo 2013 £6.99
Attractively packaged Adriatic pasta red with a dense
crimson colour and lots of bustling berry fruit; partly
oak-aged for smoothness but clean and edgy at the finish.

S. AFRICA

Y 9 Stellenbosch Drive Fairtrade Shiraz 2014 £6.99
Big, shiny, virtuous pure varietal; rich and spicy but clean
and balanced. Grand match for roasts and grills; 14.5 per
cent alcohol. Good value.

SPAIN

Y 8 Marques de Valido Rioja Reserva 2010 £8.99
Colour's pale, but this is a firm and shapely strawberry-
and-vanilla-nosed Rioja in authentic regional style.

RED WINES

SPAIN

🍷 **8 Corte Mayor Rioja Crianza 2011** £9.99
The eye-catching label serves this vigorous Baron de Ley
wine well; a plummy-spicy pure Tempranillo with evident
vanilla oak exclusive to the Co-op.

🍷 **9 Baron de Ley Rioja Reserva 2010** £10.99
Capping a nice run of Riojas, this is blood red, robust and
near-spirity in its spicy, dark pure-Tempranillo bloom of
succulent fruit.

WHITE WINES

ARGENTINA

🍷 **8 Las Moras Pinot Grigio 2014** £6.99
I like this for being riper, fuller and more interesting than
most Italian counterparts at a similar price.

AUSTRALIA

🍷 **8 Yalumba Y Series Pinot Grigio 2014** £8.49
This needs referencing more to Alsace than to Veneto. It's
exotic, smoky, full and contemplative as well as dry and
freshly appetising.

CHILE

🍷 **9 The Co-operative Truly Irresistible Leyda
Valley Sauvignon Blanc 2014** £6.99
Green gooseberry nose, zesty, emphatically grassy-nettly
fruit with benchmark Chilean generosity of ripeness and
long finish; I liked it.

🍷 **8 Montes Reserva Sauvignon Blanc 2014** £8.79
Saw-edged refresher with big seagrass blast of briny fruit
in artful balance; a food wine – oysters come easily to
mind.

WHITE WINES

🍷 9 **Domaine du Haut-Rauly Monbazillac 2013 £6.99**
Yellow-gold Dordogne pudding wine with an expensive,
Sauternes-like botrytis nose and matching ambrosial
honeyed sweetness; low on acidity but by no means
cloying, and cheap at the price if you like this sort of thing.

🍷 8 **Première Anjou Chenin Blanc 2014 £6.99**
Simple Loire dry white with a floral scent, matching
delicate fruit and a suggestion of bee-loud glade – well,
honey then. Fine aperitif with 11.5% alcohol.

🍷 8 **The Co-operative Truly Irresistible Viognier
Pays d'Oc 2014 £6.99**
Made by redoubtable Jean-Claude Mas, a lush, apricot-
scented dry-finishing food white (fish, poultry, anything
creamy) with a lick of richness.

🍷 8 **St Véran Domaine des Valanges 2014 £10.99**
Full of minty apple fruit in the proper Mâconnais
manner, a mineral-bright unoaked southern Burgundy
Chardonnay pure and long in flavour.

🍷 9 **Château Roumieu 2012 37.5cl £12.99**
Ravishingly delicious Sauternes from a top vineyard bang
next door to stellar Château Climens, already ambrosial
with sublime limey acidity in heavenly balance. Brilliant
wine from a tricky vintage. It would score top marks if
the Co-op's annual promo halves the already-fair shelf
price around Christmas.

🍷 8 **Reichsgraf von Kesselstatt Riesling
Kabinett 2011 £9.99**
Well-coloured, lively, racy and long moselle with a honey
note and a beckoning balance; 9.5% alcohol.

WHITE WINES

ITALY

🍷 **8** **The Co-operative Orvieto Classico 2014** £5.99
Once better-known than now, this gentle Umbrian off-dry wine has almondy perfume and corresponding nutty-green-fruit flavours in decent balance. Summer salads and delicate white meats.

🍷 **8** **The Co-operative Truly Irresistible Gavi Broglia 2014** £7.99
Good, even very good, example of this risingly trendy Piedmontese dry wine from Cortese grapes has full nutty style, lots of brisk orchard fruit and tangy acidity, all in balance.

N. ZEALAND

🍷 **9** **Peter Yealands Sauvignon Blanc 2014** £11.25
Zingy-nettly wildly generous ripe textbook Kiwi Sauvignon from an on-trend Marlborough maker. Smashing stuff, but quite a lot more expensive than in the excellent 2013 vintage.

SOUTH AFRICA

🍷 **8** **The Siren Fairtrade Chenin Chardonnay Viognier 2014** £5.99
Good-cause Cape mélange has fruit-salad charms in a fresh, dry and happy medium.

🍷 **8** **Stellenbosch Drive Chardonnay 2014** £6.99
Bright yellow coconut-and-peach oaked dry wine with lashings of sunny sweet-apple ripeness at a sensible price.

🍷 **10** **Thelema Sutherland Chardonnay 2012** £10.99
Thrilled to find this at the Co-op. Thelema is a legendary Stellenbosch estate and this is a fabulously lush apple-strudel Chardy barrique-made Burgundian pretender of memorable richness and poised minerality; an absolute joy at what seems a modest price.

WHITE WINES

 8 La Casa Sauvignon Blanc 2014 £6.99
This generic (Vino de la Tierra) Castilla y Leon varietal has grassy freshness and a bright Sauvignon character – tangy, but not green.

SPARKLING WINES

 10 Les Pionniers Champagne Brut £16.99
A contender for best supermarket own-label non-vintage champagne, this just seems to get more delicious every time I taste it. Mellow, developed and busily sparkling it has long brioche lemon-tipped flavours and a reassuring weightiness. The name commemorates the Rochdale Pioneers, founders of the Co-operative movement.

**9 Les Pionniers Vintage Champagne Brut
2006** £24.99
It's farewell to the fabled 2004 vintage, and hello to this successor, a golden-hued, long-bottle-aged, rich and warmly bready fizz of very evident quality. No hurry to drink it – expect more development.

Lidl

Good old Lidl. In my family we believe this to be the quirkier of the two German discounters. The stores have a cheerfully informal market feel about them, and there are always surprises among the merchandise as well as the famous perennial grocery bargains.

And then there's the wine. There's a core range of regulars I have been trying, and mostly failing to like, for years now. But in the serendipitous Lidl tradition there is also a regular flow of special wines, in limited supply, through the stores, throughout the year. They are marketed in the space now set apart in every store for the 'Cellar Selection'.

Each is rated by my good friend and Master of Wine Richard Bampfield as a guide for customers. Tastes vary of course, but Richard's expertise is formidable, and if he says a wine is well-made and honest, you can count on that. The rating scale goes up to 100 points, and it seems only wines he rates from 80 upwards get into the Cellar Selection at all. Very, very few wines reach 90 or above, so it's just about a 1-to-10 scale, really. Like mine.

My recommendation is that Lidl customers should follow Richard's lead. I tasted the last batch of Cellar Selection wines to go into the stores just before this book went to press. If there are any of them left by the time you're reading this, they do indeed come recommended.

RED WINES

CHILE

🍷 8 **Cimarosa Malbec Reserva Privada 2013**   £4.99
Plenty of black-fruit ripeness and a lick of oaky silk in this uncomplicated bargain.

FRANCE

🍷 9 **Claret Bordeaux AC 2013**   £3.99
Anonymous Cab Sauv/Merlot blend; likeable, artfully ripe, healthy and balanced and excellent value.

🍷 8 **Chevalier de Fauvert Merlot VdeP 2014**   £4.59
Plump, full, ripe southern red has juicy sweet-briar fruit and healthy balance.

🍷 9 **Serabel Côtes du Rhône Villages Chusclan 2014**   £5.99
Young purple winter red; developed briar-fruit spice with depth and savour. A smashing CdR at a great price; 14%.

🍷 8 **Domaine de l'Estagnol Minervois 2014**   £6.99
Sunnily ripe, dark and savoury-spicy Languedoc winter warmer, reassuringly well-knit and satisfying.

🍷 8 **Lussac St-Emilion 2011**   £6.99
Grippily ripe authentic elegant St Emilion style is a sleek, silky dark-fruit bargain.

🍷 8 **Jean Dumont Bourgogne Pinot Noir 2013**   £7.99
Clean, crisp, nicely weighted earthy-cherry Burgundy.

🍷 9 **Koenig Pinot Noir Réserve 2014**   £8.99
Pale but fresh Alsace with strawberry perfume and redcurrant fruit; good weight and stimulating style.

🍷 8 **Ch. Fongaban Puisseguin-Saint-Emilion 2012** £8.99
Beguiling ripe vanilla nose from this charming darkly lush claret; developed flavours nicely grippy with tannin.

RED WINES

FRANCE

8 St Emilion Grand Cru 2012   £8.99
Good generic claret from the aspirant St Emilion is
impressively opaque and intense with a meaty-plummy
perfume and lots of smoothly oaked black cherry savour.

9 Les Jablières Santenay 2014   £9.99
Proper Pinot Noir expression, juicily ripe, briskly gripping.

GERMANY

8 Dornfelder 2013   £5.49
Pale but not wan, the aroma evokes cherries, bramble-
fruit and woodshavings. This is a distinctive red wine,
juicy, summery and dry with a lick of oaky smoothness.

ITALY

8 Montepulciano d'Abruzzo 2014   £3.79
Party red with a good brambly poke and crunchy
brightness; light but not stringy.

9 Chianti Classico Fortezza dei Colli 2012   £6.99
True Chianti, attractively presented, deep maroon,
grippily fruity in the authentic manner and silkily
beguiling. It's the genuine article at a keen price.

8 Barolo 2011   £9.99
Pleasing core-range perennial; dark and dense with a
gamey savour and spicy forest-fruit pungency; 14.5%.

PORTUGAL

8 Azinhaga de Ouro Douro Reserva 2013   £5.49
'To say this wine caused a stir would be a massive
understatement', said Richard Bampfield of this red,
which he rated a rare 90 on his scale. Warmly fruity and
softly creamy with a curious lift of acidity; very cheap.

S. AFRICA

8 Cimarosa Cabernet Sauvignon 2014   £3.99
Typical everyday Cape Cabernet: warm (not stewed)
black-fruit flavours with a wholesome pungency; 14%.

RED WINES

8 **Libertario La Mancha Red 2013** £3.79
Pure Tempranillo has bouncy blackcurrant juiciness and
an elusive vanilla lick; artful contrivance at a low price.

9 **Cepa Lebrel Rioja Reserva 2009** £5.49
Easy middleweight mature blackcurranty Tempranillo
with discreet oak and lively juiciness. Worth decanting.

9 **Ribera del Duero Altos de Tamaron 2012** £5.99
Oaked wine billows with the creamy vanilla effect of
keeping new wine in cask. But young blackcurrant fruit
makes for a juicily ripe treat that tastes way above price.

9 **Vinya Carles Priorat Crianza 2010** £5.99
The mysterious dark red wines of Priorat, in remote
mountains near Barcelona, are treasured and expensive
– but here's one at an unheard-of price with gamey, spicy,
prune and liquorice depths. Worth decanting.

PINK WINES

8 **Côtes de Provence Rosé 2014** £5.99
In a designer bottle that shows off the pleasing shell-pink
colour, a delicate but assertive dry refresher.

8 **Mezquiriz Navarra Rosé 2014** £3.79
Bold magenta colour to this full-fruit raspberry-bright
dry refresher at an alluring price.

WHITE WINES

8 **Cimaroa Chardonnay 2014** £3.99
Persuasive butter, scrambled-egg oak-chardy style to a
ripe-apple wine; artfully plausible, especially at the price.

SPAIN · FRANCE · SPAIN · AUS.

WHITE WINES

CHILE

8 **Cimarosa Pedro Jimenez 2014** £3.99
Floral nose, dry muscat-like fruit, fresh and interesting.

FRANCE

9 **Grand Fief de Retail Muscadet
Sèvre et Maine Sur Lie 2014** £5.99
Nuanced crisply zesty Loire-estuary mussel-matcher is
safely this side of green but tangily fresh and delicious.

8 **Le Cellier Savoyard Apremont 2014** £6.49
Tangy dry white from Savoie has racy-grassy appeal.

8 **Mâcon-Villages Les Chanussots 2014** £6.79
Brisk bright mineral Chardonnay in the best Mâcon
tradition at a fair if not exceptional price.

8 **Koenig Riesling Réserve 2014** £7.99
Nice tight Alsace wine, dry and apple-crisp with long
aromatic flavours; good example.

9 **Bourgogne Hautes-Côtes de Nuits** £8.99
A shade riper and earthier than its Beaune counterpart
above, a seductive Burgundy of real charm.

8 **Bourgogne Hautes-Côtes de Beaune** £8.99
Remarkable mineral-bright and racy white Burgundy of
real character; I simply can't fault it.

8 **Chablis 2013** £8.99
Another successful vintage for this core wine, notably
flinty and citrus on the nose and copious in mineral
flavours; tastes as Chablis should. Not cheap, but sound.

8 **Reuilly Cuvée Prestige Fiefs des Comelias 2014** £8.99
Rare and ritzy Loire Valley Sauvignon, abundant with
seagrass lushness; brisk but long in stony-pure flavours.

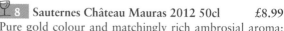

WHITE WINES

FRANCE

🍷 8 **Sauternes Château Mauras 2012 50cl**　　£8.99
Pure gold colour and matchingly rich ambrosial aroma;
easy weight of honeyed fruit.

GERMANY

🍷 8 **Riesling Feinherb Mosel 2014**　　£4.99
Sad there is so little Rhine or Mosel wine in this German
giant's list but this grapy-racy Brauneberger Kurfürstlay
is a nod in the right direction; 10.5% alcohol.

🍷 9 **Junge Rheingauer Riesling 2013**　　£7.99
Dry, racy and limey Rheingau Riesling is a force of nature,
well able to match white meats and poultry.

N.Z.

🍷 8 **Cimarosa Marlborough Sauvignon Blanc 2014** £5.89
Entry-level wine, grassy and brisk in the Kiwi manner
with a lemon edge to the lively fruit.

SPAIN

🍷 8 **Conde Noble White Wine 2013**　　£2.99
Dry, brassica-green cooking white – the cheapest entry of
the year and really not that bad; 11% alcohol.

SPARKLING WINES

🍷 8 **Comte de Senneval Champagne Brut**　　£9.97
Biscuity-yeasty, fresh and foaming – it tastes right so it
must be champagne, even at this unheard-of price.

FRANCE

🍷 8 **Champagne Bissinger Grand Prestige Brut** £15.99
Mellow and brightly fresh, terrific at the price. Richard
Bampfield scored it at 91.

🍷 8 **Champagne Bissinger Brut Rosé**　　£16.99
Lively fizzy strawberry-nosed and pinkly poised
champagne with a sweet dosage just short of OTT.

Majestic

All change at Majestic. Early in 2015 the 212-branch 'warehouse' chain parted with chief executive Steve Lewis, who had worked there for 29 years, over worries about a profits downturn. The company then bought Naked Wines, an online subscription retailer, for £70 million. Rowan Gormley, who founded Naked in 2008, was appointed Majestic's new chief executive. In June, Majestic announced a drop in profits of 22 per cent over the previous year. Mr Gormley has plans to put things right. A strategic review is under way which, according to one investment analyst, 'confirms our belief that there are material self-help levers which can drive volumes, improve returns and unlock working capital inefficiencies'.

So that's all right, then. Meanwhile, how are the wines at Majestic? I'll tell you one thing. There are a lot fewer of them than there used to be. In the everyday range, that is. The 'fine wine' offering seems to be flourishing, but is not, sadly, within the remit of this book. Majestic appears here among the supermarkets because it has to date been a realistic rival to them. I await developments.

As ever, a cautionary word about the prices quoted here. Majestic's policy of periodical multibuy discounts on a major proportion of its list means that many of the wines I describe will actually cost you 25 or even 33 per cent under the figure quoted. To qualify, you just have to buy two bottles as part of the minimum six-bottle purchase.

That said, I gather that the minimum-purchase and discount policies are now under review. Again, I await developments.

RED WINES

ARGENTINA

8 Hey Malbec! 2013 £14.99

Dramatic dark purple colour and expressive savoury-juicy black fruit emerge very likeably from this puzzlingly expensive and very oddly presented Mendoza pure varietal; 14.5% alcohol.

AUSTRALIA

9 The Lodge Hill Shiraz 2012 £14.99

From the Clare Valley's Jim Barry, an old friend on fine form living up to the label's own evocation of 'rosemary, black plum and cumin' in the aromas and flavours of a long, soothing and savoury classic Shiraz, made the proper way; 14.5% alcohol.

8 Gnarly Dudes Shiraz 2013 £23.00

Deep, deep purple Barossa fruit bomb of real depth and intensity but all in fine balance; 15% alcohol.

FRANCE

9 Côtes du Rhône Les Fustiers 2014 £9.99

Name makes it sound a bit superannuated, but this is a bright, perky and spicy Côtes du Rhône of lively juiciness with body and intensity. Really liked it.

8 Beaujolais-Villages Georges Duboeuf 2012 £9.99

Restyled label, but still dependable mellow, full-of-fruit, juicy, everyday Beaujolais in the familiar manner; this one's old, but fun.

8 Domaine de Montval Syrah 2014 £9.99

Pays du Gard has a warm brambly whiff, expressive wild black fruit and a tinge of white pepper; works well.

RED WINES

9 Mas du Colombel Faugères 2013   £11.99

The Mediterranean hill-country AC of Faugères makes
distinctively spicy, fruits-of-the-forest reds with dark
elements of liquorice and roasty savour – just like this
deep dark purple winter warmer with sturdy intensity;
14% alcohol.

8 Magellan Pinot Noir 2014   £11.99

A pays d'Oc made by the Lafon family of Burgundy, an
un-burgundy-like Pinot nevertheless of earthy charm
with ripe strawberry fruit tautly poised and bright; really
enjoyable.

8 Château Greysac 2008   £14.99

Majestic regular Médoc cru bourgeois in its maturity has
a beckoning perfume that speaks clearly of claret and
the right kind of cassis-cedar-minty dark fruit; nice easy
weight.

8 Vacqueyras Les Hauts de la Ponche 2013   £19.99

Premium Rhône red, robust, pruny-ripe and intense
with proper regional spice and grip; still young it has
propitious savour and length; 14.5% alcohol.

8 Châteauneuf du Pape Mont Redon
       Vignoble Abeille 2010   £28.00

Hate to brag but I have lately tried a 1961 Mont Redon
(thank you, Robin Yapp) and found it heavenly; this
dark, nuanced and ripe successor is looking good and
will certainly repay keeping 10 years if not 50; 14.5%
alcohol.

FRANCE

RED WINES

FRANCE

🍷 8 **Louis Latour Gevrey-Chambertin 2007**   £30.00
Big-name village burgundy at a scary price turns out a
gem: lovely strawberry perfume and silky-clingy brisk
Pinot Noir fruit perfectly poised in its earthy-gamey
maturity; show-off's wine but an experience.

🍷 8 **Natale Verga Primitivo 2014**   £8.99
This unexpectedly delicate and juicy red-berry spaghetti
wine from Puglia has poise and succulence.

ITALY

🍷 8 **Aglianico del Vulture Cantina di Venosa
2012**   £9.99
Toasty, spicy but smooth food red from Basilicata's
happily named ex-volcano Vulture – gripping but
comfortable drinking; 14% alcohol.

🍷 9 **Maretti Langhe Rosso 2013**   £11.99
I am accustomed to generic Langhe (Piedmont) reds made
from Nebbiolo, the grape of Barolo. This one is seven
parts Barbera to three of Nebbiolo but I love it just the
same: dark, juicy, bouncing and vigorous and very much
the sum of its noble parts.

NEW ZEALAND

🍷 8 **Belmont Pinot Noir 2014**   £11.99
Straight minty-raspberry proper Kiwi (Nelson) red with
firmness and edge.

🍷 8 **Selaks Reserve Merlot Cabernet 2013**   £15.99
Bordeaux blend which delivers the expected cassis,
blackberry and cherry fruit but with added Kiwi sleekness,
bounce and muscularity; distinctively relishable; 14%
alcohol.

RED WINES

N. ZEALAND

9 **Martinborough Vineyard Te Tera Pinot Noir 2013** £19.99
From the vineyard that pioneered Kiwi Pinot a sumptuous creamy lush summer-pudding red of perfectly defined fruit and long flavours, finishing lipsmackingly bright and clean.

PORTUGAL

8 **Porta 6 2012** £9.99
This Lisboa red from mainly Port grapes has a trademark Portuguese dark clove and spice black-fruit savour; substantial and satisfying. Heed not the ghastly label.

SOUTH AFRICA

10 **Graham Beck Antony's Yard 2013** £9.99
Slinky Cabernet-Merlot blend, clearly inspired by the poised and elegant Bordeaux formula, but you don't get claret this ripe, balanced and wholesome even at £9.99 let alone the £6.66 deal prevailing at time of tasting; a delicious bargain; 14.5% alcohol.

9 **Jordan Cabernet Merlot 2011** £10.99
Another Bordeaux-style blend with southern hemisphere extra ripeness and roundness but still in fine balance, made by one of the Cape's great estates; 14.5% alcohol.

SPAIN

8 **Bienbebido Queso Tempranillo 2012** £9.99
Plump blackcurranty healthy party red.

8 **Finca Carelio Tempranillo 2011** £9.99
Intense and gripping black-fruit winter warmer to drink with spicy sausage; 14.5% alcohol.

RED WINES

9 Muriel Rioja Reserva Vendimia Seleccionada 2010   £10.65

The alleged price is £10.65 which just happens to morph into £7.99 with the 25% discount if you buy two. I point this out, even though the same could be said about nearly every other wine in this section, because this one's a cracker. Smartly packaged, richly intense creamy-spikily juicy classic Rioja all the way through.

8 Marqués de Cacarés Rioja Gran Reserva 2008   £22.00

Princely new-oaked high-toned still vigorous cerebral wine with a long future and an attention-grabbing present, too. A handsome brute.

SPAIN

PINK WINES

8 Miraval Rosé 2014   £17.99

About as good as rosé gets, a coral coloured, delicately soft-summer-fruits-scented very dry and fresh Côtes de Provence wine expertly made by someone other than the estate's owners, Mr and Mrs Brad Pitt.

7 AIX Rosé 2014 1.5l   £19.99

Eye-catching magnum bottle shows off the glowing salmon colour to good effect; a discreetly sweet, clean and pink-tasting Coteaux d'Aix en Provence wine for blingy parties.

8 M de Minuty Rosé 2014 1.5l   £25.00

In an amphora-shaped magnum bottle, another salmon-coloured Provence pink, drier, crisper and more pleasing than the AIX above. Standard bottles are £14.99 but promo price for 2 was £9.99 at the time.

FRANCE

PINK WINES

N. ZEALAND

8 **Black Cottage Rosé 2014** £12.99
Smoked-salmon coloured Pinot Gris and Pinot Noir mix
with lots of fruity-berry flavour and a positive crispness.

WHITE WINES

CHILE

8 **Days of Summer 2014** £9.99
Cryptic brand by Miguel Torres is a dry Muscat with
masses of grapey fruit that thoroughly refreshes; artful
and likeable.

8 **Viña Mayu Dry Pedro Ximenez 2014** £10.49
Aromatic and indeed dry refresher from Elqui Valley;
stays in the mind.

FRANCE

9 **Pierre-Jean Sauvion Chenin Blanc 2014** £8.99
A mere 'vin de France' but this delightful aperitif wine
travels from the freshest of entries via a sublime balance
to a honeyed centre and twangy-bright finish; 11.5%
alcohol.

9 **Villemarin Picpoul de Pinet 2014** £8.99
This feels weightier than other examples of this trendy
Languedoc dry wine I have come across this year; lots of
ripe white fruit and a ting of citrus.

8 **Domaine Ferrandière Riesling 2014** £8.99
How's this? A Riesling Pays d'Oc by all-encompassing
Midi maestro Paul Mas. It's Riesling all right, racy, appley
and almost fiercely dry – nothing like the Alsace version,
but not an unwelcome new idea.

WHITE WINES

8 Domaine Sainte Ferréol Viognier 2013 £9.99
Lots of Viognier around this year, among them this plump
and marrowy Pays d'Oc with dried-apricot perfume and
a cleverly clean and snappy liveliness; stands out.

**8 Bourgogne Chardonnay Les Chenaudières
2014 £10.99**
Agreeable buttery scrambled egg nose (well, just a
suggestion of it) and lush fresh Chardonnay fruit from
the Cave de Lugny in the Mâconnais.

8 Chablis Domaine Servin 2014 £14.99
Steely lemony style for grown-ups – pure, unoaked and
delicious.

9 Clos St Jacques Gewürztraminer 2011 £17.99
Bumper gold Alsace wine has a big lychee perfume and a
rush of deeply spicy exotic but brisk textbook autumn-
ripe fruit; very nicely made at the Domaine de la Ville de
Colmar and 15% alcohol, no less.

9 L'Etoile de Begude Chardonnay 2013 £17.99
Organically made oaked Chardonnay of Limoux, close to
the Pyrenees, with a rich colour and matching ripe sweet-
apple fruit balanced by bright minerality and a nice limey
acidity; intriguing and well-made.

7 Pouilly-Fumé Jonathan Pabiot 2014 £19.99
Grand but expensive Loire classic jumps with grassy, even
smoky, Sauvignon twang.

FRANCE

WHITE WINES

Majestic

FRANCE

8 **Saint-Aubin 1er Cru Gérard Thomas et Filles 2013** £25.00

This lushly oaked Beaune has creamy apple depths and an expensive lemon glitter.

8 **Araldica Cortese 2014** £7.99

Zesty green-fruit Piedmont wine from the grape that makes Gavi, this has an attractive blanched-almond richness; 11.5% alcohol.

ITALY

8 **Pietrariccia Fiano 2014** £9.99

Crisp Puglian take on the now-familiar Fiano theme, fresh and orchardy, featuring both a nutty richness and fine-tuned citrus acidity.

8 **Pasqua Passimento Bianco 2014** £11.99

Sweet-apple background to an off-dry rather impressive aperitif wine from Garganega (Soave) grapes, some of them dried to a concentrated state before fermentation.

NEW ZEALAND

8 **Invivo Sauvignon Blanc 2014** £13.49

Impactful nettly number from Awatere, Marlborough, this is lively and long.

8 **Waimea Estate Pinot Gris 2014** £14.99

Plump, smoky PG contrives a dry freshness but also delivers on the exotic spiciness you expect.

PORTUGAL

8 **Casal de Ventozela Vinho Verde 2014** £9.99

Quite dry but with a crafty sweetness to the raspy green fruit and a tingle of pétillance.

WHITE WINES

S. AFRICA

🍷 8 **Rachel's Chenin Blanc 2014** £8.99
A very green label, but not a green wine; florally scented,
ripely refreshing dry food matcher (fish to poultry) by
Boschendal with purpose and shape; 14% alcohol.

SPAIN

🍷 9 **Martin Codax As Caixas Godello 2014** £9.99
Big dry sea-fresh crisp white food white from rising-
star varietal Godello produced in breezy Galicia by the
region's top co-operative Martin Codax – good lemon
tang to finish makes this a fine shellfish match.

USA

🍷 8 **Chateau Saint Jean Chardonnay 2013** £12.99
The name of this Californian North Coast winery alludes
perhaps to Burgundian pretensions, but this feels bigger
and riper than that; impressive lush fruit lit by mineral
freshness.

🍷 8 **Rickshaw Chardonnay 2014** £15.99
Part-barrel-fermented Californian wine has apple-pie
richness and a bit of regional glitter; try not to be put off
by the gimmicky package; 14% alcohol.

SPARKLING WINES

ENGLAND

🍷 8 **Balfour 1503 Brut** £29.99

From the spiffing-sounding Hush Heath estate, a manor founded in 1503, a decidely tangy and fresh proper sparkler from champagne varieties; genuinely good. I would like to drink it with fish and chips, seriously.

FRANCE

🍷 8 **L'Extra par Langlois Crémant de Loire Brut** £14.99

Vivacious Chenin Blanc with busy sparkle, crisp but creamy white fruit; not ersatz champagne, a fine fizz in its own right.

─Marks & Spencer─

Browsing the wine sections in the M&S stores that fall within my shopping range, I am always impressed with their compactness. The displays seem very much less conspicuous than those of the big supermarkets' vast wine departments. This might give the impression that the choice of wine at M&S is comparatively limited.

Not a bit of it. The range is vast, and easily as varied as that of any other grocery retailer (except Waitrose). There are wines from all over. Where else can you get, for example, offerings from Arbois or Savoie in the Alps, from Brazil and India? Or real Lambrusco and Vinho Verde? One of my top finds at M&S this year comes from Uruguay. And if English wines are your choice, M&S is unmatched.

All the wines bear the M&S imprint. No space is wasted on universal brands. Prices are fair and there are regular instore promotions, often on the multibuy principle of buy six bottles get x per cent off the lot.

M&S has an excellent dedicated wine website offering the whole range in six-bottle cases. It's a handy way of perusing the full choice, as the great variation in the size of M&S stores means a corresponding inconsistency in the wine selection. Another attraction online: buy any two six-bottle cases together and you get 25 per cent off. It always says this is a time-limited offer, but it always seems to be there.

RED WINES

Marks & Spencer

ARGENTINA

9 **Butcher's Block Bonarda-Malbec 2014**   £6.00
Argentina's Malbec makers seem anxious to connect this macho grape's appeal with the eating of beef. This wine is, though, 70% Bonarda and just 30% Malbec, and while sturdy enough its appeal comes from the eager brambly bounce of the blackberry fruit; bargain.

8 **Caleidoscopio Malbec Touriga Nacional Mourvèdre 2014**   £8.00
Quirky blend from Santa Julia winery makes a generous summer-pudding-fruit barbecue red with long flavours and a firm finish.

8 **Dominio del Plata Terroir Series Malbec 2014**   £12.00
Deep purple Mendoza wine, tensely silky and darkly spicy showing real varietal virtue, already developed with a sweet tannic grip; a class act at 14.5% alcohol.

AUSTRALIA

8 **Pichi Richi Shiraz 2014**   £7.00
Dark gently spicy juicily blackberry-ripe barbecue red in sophisticated balance by De Bortoli; 14% alcohol.

8 **6285 Margaret River Merlot 2014**   £10.00
Hugely ripe morello-cherry monster of cushiony plumpness, skilfully balanced by clingy clean tannin edge and artful acidity. So well-made; 14% alcohol.

9 **Ebenezer & Seppeltsfield Shiraz 2012**   £15.00
Seductive sweetly-oaked and wildly black-fruit Christmas Day wine from Chateau Tanunda in the Barossa – worth every penny; 14.5% alcohol.

RED WINES

CHILE

🍷 8 **La Huasa Merlot 2014** £8.50
Overt black-cherry fruit of controlled sweetness and spicy
tannins wrapping up the long, dark surge of flavours;
Chilean Merlot as it should be.

FRANCE

🍷 9 **Gamay Vin de Pays de L'Ardèche 2014** £6.00
Return to form for this juicy purple refresher from the
grape of Beaujolais grown in neighbouring Ardèche; best
vintage since 2008 according to my insistent notes.

🍷 8 **Château Gillet Bordeaux 2014** £7.50
Appealing young Entre-Deux-Mers claret which is
already sunny ripe and wholesome with a leafy vigour
as well as dark berry fruit; the tannin is firm but gentle.

🍷 7 **Beaujolais 2014** £8.50
Juicy-bouncy textbook young Beaujolais of genuine
charm and authenticity by very-long-term supplier to
M&S Paul Sapin; for a basic AC wine it seems expensive.

🍷 9 **Domaine de la Meynarde Plan de Dieu**
Côtes du Rhône Villages 2014 £9.00
Plush and poised, this is a superbly taut and spicy Côtes
du Rhône, a beacon afloat on what can be a sea of
mediocrity; it is unoaked but has a plump completeness
very much its own; 14% alcohol.

🍷 8 **Lirac Les Closiers 2013** £10.00
Silky and substantial young unoaked Rhône with darkly
ripe berry fruit and lingering juiciness; got it for £6 in an
in-store promo; 14% alcohol.

RED WINES

FRANCE

8 **Les Voiles de Paulilles Collioure 2013** £12.00
Focused briary Grenache-based richly ripe rarity from
the Pyrenean southwest will impress with its vigour and
savoury content.

GERMANY

10 **Palataia Pinot Noir 2013** £10.00
Made by former M&S buyer Gerd Stepp in the Rheinpalz/
Palatinate this lovely raspberry-juicy, bouncing Pinot
has lushness of fruit and ideal refreshing abrasiveness;
eager summer soft fruits abound in the long, committed
flavours; a fine match for game birds and poultry, or cool
as a summer sipper.

GREECE

8 **Red on Black 2013** £9.00
Cryptically named perhaps, but this substantial wine
from Agiorgitiko is easy to enjoy for its blackcurranty
flush of fruit and lipsmacking dry finish.

ITALY

10 **Toscana Rosso 2012** £6.00
Miraculous Chianti-style juice bomb with cherry-ripe
plump fruit from Sangiovese fortified with Cabernet
Sauvignon and Merlot, making an artful bargain for
pasta meals and barbecues.

9 **Beneventano Aglianico 2013** £6.50
Worthy successor to fine 2011 vintage (2012 seems to
have been passed over) a densely dark spicy-savoury
blackberry juice bomb from the Campania; a natural
match for well-seasoned tomato-based pasta. Good value.

8 **Negroamaro 2013** £7.50
From San Marzano in Puglia, dark and spicy red-meat
red with a whiff of volcanic ardour and a bitter chocolate
centre.

RED WINES

8 Valpolicella Valpantena 2014 £8.00

Top-drawer Verona wine with unexpected density of colour and cherry-raspberry fruit intensity; wildly fruity and vivid match for the more delicate pasta dishes.

9 Lambrusco Secco Reggiano £9.00

This is real Lambrusco (named after the constituent black grape variety), technically a sparkling wine but only marginally so; it's deep purple, wildly perfumed and jumping with briary fresh hedgerow fruit flavours all rushing to the tastebuds in a foaming rather than fizzing flood. Drink it chilled, with or without suitable Italian antipasto; 11% alcohol.

8 Valpolicella Ripasso 2013 £9.50

Verona's famous cherry-and-almond red souped up with wine from dried grapes is grippingly good; concentrated black fruit marries well with the natural sweetness.

9 Aglianico del Vulture 2013 £10.00

The name of this wine alone is sufficient to inspire, and the bumper, pitch-dark spicy-brimstone black-fruit flavours, robed in a warming caramel richness and finishing very dry, fully live up to expectations.

8 Nicosia Etna Rosso 2013 £10.00

Splendid Sicilian red sporting a label featuring Etna's volcano in fierce eruption; the wine is bright ruby, leafy, spicy and warm with bright berry fruits and really rather elegant in its weight.

RED WINES

9 Renato Ratti Langhe Nebbiolo 2011   £14.00

Made by a famed and delightfully named Barolo producer, this M&S perennial filled this space last year so here it is again in the same excellent vintage: limpid colour just browning a tinge, strawberry-spirity-creamy Barolo-like nose, lush intense ripe cherry fruit in silky texture; 14% alcohol.

8 Stellenrust Pinotage 2014   £9.00

Tar and spice in the customary Pinotage manner feature in this Fairtrade pure varietal with controlled ripeness and warmth; 14% alcohol.

8 Paul Cluver Ferricrete Pinot Noir 2014   £12.00

Pale and slinky Pinot earthily interesting and soft-summer-fruit lush, from iron-oxide-rich shale in the Elgin region known as ferricrete or, more picturesquely 'koffieklip' (coffee soil) in Afrikaans.

8 Las Falleras Tinto 2014   £5.25

From Bobal grapes of the Utiel-Requena region a brightly purple raspberry-ripe summer red with juiciness and zest; charming and cheap.

8 Raso de la Cruz Tinto 2014   £7.00

This Garnacha and Tempranillo blend from the Cariñena region is brambly and fresh with a firm grip of friendly tannin and, unexpectedly, just 10% alcohol.

8 Organic Old Vine Tempranillo 2014   £8.00

Startling crimson cassis-ripe tastebud grabber from high-altitude Uclés region, bright with blackcurrant juiciness; 14% alcohol.

RED WINES

URUGUAY

🍷 10 **Pisano Cisplatino Tannat 2014**   £9.00
Great wines pop up in unexpected places. The Tannat grape, famed for its antioxidant properties more than its vinous merits, is here grown in Uruguay's South Atlantic province of Progreso to make an exceptional red, soupy crimson in colour, expansive in evolved plummy-juicy-berry fruit that well outstrips the oak influence in richness and balances beautifully. Gorgeous winter red that tastes way above its price.

USA

🍷 8 **Underwood Pinot Noir 2013**   £13.00
Pale, gently browning Oregon wine, sweetly lush with oak-contact richness and elegantly poised; it has a distinctive earthy charm that might just be an Oregon trait.

WHITE WINES

ARGENTINA

🍷 8 **Fisherman's Catch Chenin Blanc 2014**   £6.00
Good-value party white offers perky green freshness with a honey trace.

AUSTRALIA

🍷 8 **Pichi Richi Chardonnay 2014**   £7.00
Healthy New South Wales Chardy by De Bortoli has a lick of oaky coconut and lively appley freshness.

🍷 8 **6285 Margaret River Chardonnay 2014**   £13.00
Immediately impressive wine balancing plump sweet ripeness with mineral purity; lobster would be a suitable accompaniment.

WHITE WINES

8 Araucaria Riesling Pinot Grigio 2014 £9.00
Crowd-pleasing blend introduced in time for the 2016
Olympics in Rio, quite dry and lively with racy orchard
fruits; 11.5% alcohol.

9 Tierra Y Hombre Sauvignon Blanc 2014 £8.50
Perennial Casablanca favourite is bracing, briny and bold
in all the best ways, a modern, well-intentioned Sauvignon
comparable for quality and value with Marlborough
counterparts.

8 Cascara Limari Valley Chardonnay 2013 £8.50
Straightforward unoaked, sweet-apple, sunny, pure
varietal of a kind I identify closely with Chile; wholesome.

8 Emiliana Organic Viognier 2014 £10.00
From (relatively) cool-climate Casablanca Valley, a dry
food white (poultry as well as fish) with exotic fruit
flavours; unusually interesting for Viognier; 14.5%
alcohol.

**9 Côtes du Rhône Villages Réserve du Boulas
Laudun 2014** £9.00
You don't see a lot of white Côtes du Rhône in
supermarkets, and I strongly recommend this one: fruit-
salad flavours in a friskily brisk context of freshness;
nuanced dry wine comparable with expensive white
Châteauneuf du Pape.

**9 Touraine Sauvignon Blanc Domaine
Jacky Marteau 2014** £9.00
Interesting mélange of green fruits in this gooseberry-
tangy, nettly-fresh Loire wine whose appeal is extended
by palpable ripeness and length of flavour.

BRAZIL

CHILE

FRANCE

Marks & Spencer

WHITE WINES

🍷 8 **Fête du Gris Sauvignon Gris 2014**   £9.00
Vin de Pays d'Oc by leading regional co-operative Foncalieu is very like a crisp, grassy Sauvignon Blanc but with an added element of smokiness; intriguingly enjoyable.

🍷 8 **Savoie Blanc Coeur Terroir 2014**   £9.00
This Alpine dry white will be familiar to skiers and possibly mistaken for Muscadet; green-apple fruit, tangy and breezy-bright it does indeed evoke its mountainous heartland; 11% alcohol.

🍷 8 **Lo Abarca Riesling 2013**   £10.00
Think Aussie-style Riesling rather than German: fresh and tangy on first taste, with ripe green-apple tang and near-sweet grapiness at the finish. Rieslingophiles should try this.

🍷 8 **Chablis Domaine de Préhy 2011**   £14.50
Nose of authentic sweet-green ripeness from this Jean Marc Brocard item is nicely followed up in the crisp gunflint flavours and evolved intensity; very proper Chablis.

🍷 8 **Domaine de la Pinte Arbois Chardonnay 2011**   £16.00
Exotic Alpine dry pure varietal with rich colour, nutty-creamy Chardonnay aroma and luxuriant apple-pie fruit. Special-occasion wine of real mineral clarity.

🍷 9 **Palatia Pinot Grigio 2014**   £9.50
From the Pfalz or 'Palatinate' of the Rhine a definingly crisp and bracing PG with exotic smoke and spice but above all zest and freshness; best PG of the year.

WHITE WINES

GERMANY

🍷 10 **Mineralstein Riesling 2014** £10.00
Aptly named Rhine thriller jangling with crisp-apple,
pure-racy-Riesling fruit with a lemon tang and a ghost of
grapey richness; a lively, stimulating food wine made by
former in-house M&S winemaker Gerd Stepp, now with
his own winery in the Pfalz.

GREECE

🍷 8 **Atlantis Santorini 2013** £10.50
Holiday dry white from chic island resort, made of
ubiquitous Hellenic grape Assyrtiko, here masquerading
as Sauvignon, fresh, structured and grassy. Drink this,
save Greece!

INDIA

🍷 8 **Jewel of Nasik Sauvignon Blanc 2014** £7.00
Near-austere new vintage of this Bombay oddity; it's the
first Sauvignon in my book to evoke globe artichoke, and
I mean that kindly; unusual and likeable.

ITALY

🍷 8 **Bianco Terre Siciliane 2014** £6.50
Brisk Grillo-Catarratto mix with a little leesy almond
richness amid the ripe green freshness.

🍷 8 **Pecorino Umani Ronchi 2014** £10.00
M&S was first among the big grocers with this quaintly
named varietal from Marche and it is consistently
distinctive with rich colour, exotic stone-fruit aroma and
long, fresh dry flavours, citrus-edged.

N. ZEALAND

🍷 9 **Craft 3 Marlborough Sauvignon Blanc
2014** £11.00
Made by an M&S team of three, an up-range Sauvignon
of full fruit, nettly zest and bright green flavours; exciting
quality.

WHITE WINES

N. ZEALAND

8 **Saint Clair James Sinclair Sauvignon Blanc**
2014 **£16.00**
Lovely leesy long luxury Marlborough wine for Kiwi fans
anxious to try everything; quite expensive.

PORTUGAL

10 **Tapada de Villar Vinho Verde 2014** **£8.00**
I've been waiting for one of these for years: a truly spiky-
dry 'green wine' of the Minho Valley as distinct from the
sweetened garbage the Minhoans have been sending us
for decades. You get a nice little spritz, a really prickly
attack of crisp white fruit and plenty of tang. It's the real
thing, even though the maker admits to 6gm of residual
sugar per litre; 10.5% alcohol. Top Marks!

SOUTH AFRICA

8 **Cape White 2015** **£5.25**
Pure Chenin Blanc from the Mediterranean climes of the
Western Cape, crisply green in fruit with the trademark
Chenin honey note and convincingly fresh.

8 **Ken Forrester Workhorse Chenin Blanc**
2014 **£8.50**
Quite strict in its bracing dryness, a distinctive food wine
(Asian, white fish, rice dishes) with a rush of ripe green
fruit enriched with an oak presence; 14% alcohol.

SPAIN

8 **House White Wine 2014** **£5.25**
Intriguing dry white pure Macabeo from Valencia has
elements of brassica and herbaceousness as well as easy
freshness and even a twitch of nectar; 11.5% alcohol.
Fun, and cheap.

WHITE WINES

SPAIN

Ɣ 8 Raso de la Cruz Blanco 2014   £7.00
Macabeo again (see immediately above), this time from
Cariñena, is grassy and refreshing with a clear lemon
twang.

SPARKLING WINES

ENGLAND

Ɣ 8 Langham Estate Brut Rosé   £23.00
Fine onion-skin colour, bright strawberry and citrus
aroma and likeable corresponding fruit in this luxury
sparkler from Dorset, from Pinot Noir and other
champagne varieties.

8 Marksman Brut Blanc de Blancs 2010   £26.00
On-target pure-Chardonnay from Ridgeview in Sussex is
lively but mellow, very much in the champagne manner
and at a champagne price.

FRANCE

Ɣ 8 Oudinot Brut   £25.00
M&S's stalwart house blanc de blancs champagne is
dependably creamy with arch apple fruit and evident
mellowness from bottle age.

ITALY

Ɣ 8 Ferrari Brut   £20.00
Terrific all-Chardonnay, bottle-fermented proper fizz
from the Trentino region is lively with appley fruit,
bakery-evoking on the nose and long in flavour; great
fun. Note on nomenclature: Ferrari fizz was founded in
1902, the famous motor marque in 1929.

Morrisons

Morrisons is, I suppose, playing catch-up. Each of its larger rivals among the Big Four supermarkets has firmly established the style and content of its own-label wine range, and Morrisons must compete.

They're doing a good job. The 'Signature' mid-price wine range features prominently in the following pages, and the entry-level Morrisons own-label wines likewise. Many of the latter are priced under £6 or even under £5. Morrisons Côtes du Rhône at £4.75 is one of my bargains of the year.

Mark Jarman, in charge of wine at Morrisons, wishes to 'make sure our own brand is the best in the market' and reveals that 'our buyers personally blend 90 per cent of our wines at source'. This certainly shows determination to give the Morrisons offering a style of its own. The own-label wines I have tasted reflect this.

The wine departments in the store have become more spacious and prominent in recent years, and there are – inevitably – regular price promotions. There are good deals to be had too on the Morrisons Cellar section of the main website from which you can pick and mix your own case of individual bottles from across the range.

RED WINES

Argentina

🍷 8   **Alzar Malbec 2014**   £7.49
Well-made, sinewy but not tough, black-hearted unoaked but smoothly textured red-meat wine by Trivento.

🍷 9   **Viñalba Reservado de la Familia Malbec 2012**   £9.99
Coal and leather, to my way of sniffing it, come off this wine very alluringly, followed up by black savoury fruit with prune and liquorice in the depths, but it's an uplifting balanced wine all the way; 14.5% alcohol.

🍷 8   **La Posta Bonarda 2013**   £9.99
Interesting Italian-style Mendoza red gives dark ripeness and oaked richness to the juicy, vigorous plummy-berry fruit, finishing briskly dry, also in the Italian manner.

Australia

🍷 8   **M Signature Barossa Shiraz 2013**   £6.99
Concentrated spicy-savoury dark-hearted varietal includes a measure of Viognier, perhaps adding a lift to the fruit that gives this a pleasing weight.

🍷 8   **M Signature Limestone Coast Cabernet Sauvignon 2013**   £7.49
Likeable, expansive but not over-ripe, traditional Aussie Cabernet with cushiony blackcurrant fruit and a corrective acidity.

Chile

🍷 9   **Marques De Casa Concha Syrah 2012**   £11.99
Luxury pure varietal by Concha y Toro is deep in purple colour and spicy with blackberry ripe fruit too; lush vanilla oak treatment by no means overwhelms the piquancy of the fruit – it's all in fine balance; 14.5% alcohol.

RED WINES

CHILE

 10 **Valdivieso Single Vineyard Cabernet Franc 2010**   £13.99

These Valdivieso single vineyard wines are fantastic, demonstrating the scary talents of Chile's best winemakers to wondrous effect. This one shows the inimitable stalky-leafy tinge of greenness of the Cabernet Franc and elegantly marries it to a silky suppleness of red fruit (there's a noticeable 10% of sweet black-fruit Merlot in the mix) that thrills the senses; 14% alcohol. The one trouble is that's available online only.

FRANCE

 8 **Morrisons Claret 2013**   £4.49

Healthy Merlot, light but not lean and bright with blackberry fruit. 'Brilliant with bangers' says the label.

 10 **Morrisons Côtes du Rhône**   £4.75

Really pleasing 70% Grenache/30% Syrah blend from 2012 and 2014 vintages, full of vigorous fruit and controlled spiciness, satisfying in weight and altogether thoroughly wholesome; at under a fiver an outstanding bargain.

 8 **M Signature Beaujolais Villages 2014**   £6.49

Frisky, juicy, purple, properly-made characterful Beaujolais best served cool, at least in the warmer parts of the year.

 8 **M Signature Red Burgundy 2015**   £7.99

Jolly interesting mix of 7 parts Pinot Noir with 3 of Gamay from the rated Beaujolais cru of Morgon; makes a quite-sturdy but brightly juicy summer-red-fruit wine of substance and length.

RED WINES

Morrisons

FRANCE

9 **Château l'Argenteyre 2010** £12.99
Classic Médoc cru bourgeois from a legendary vintage now coming round. Has a strong ruby colour, fine cassis-cigar-box-violets nose, silky but taut dark blackberry fruit of rounding ripeness; 14% alcohol. A very classy claret for the money.

8 **Eric Louis Sancerre Rouge La Côte Blanche 2013** £14.99
This rare red from the famed Loire appellation is pure Pinot Noir with some of the keen minerality of the locality but sleekly oaked to warm and smooth the ripe cherry-raspberry fruit.

ITALY

8 **M Signature Nero d'Avola 2014** £5.49
Warming dark-hearted clovey-spicy-briary Sicilian winter red with long flavours and good grip.

8 **M Signature Montepulciano d'Abruzzo 2013** £5.99
Easy brambly midweight with a little richness from oak ageing and a good piquancy of plucked fruit in there too.

8 **M Signature Sangiovese Superiore 2013** £5.99
From the lost plains of the Emilia-Romagna, a Chianti-like intense, cherry-raspberry ripe and well-knit satisfying pasta red of unanticipated togetherness.

8 **I Crinali Nero di Troia 2013** £7.49
Darkly pungent roasted black-fruit Puglian red to match meaty pasta dishes.

RED WINES

ITALY

🍷 7 **The Wanted Zin 2013** £9.49

The bizarre name derives from the belief that Zin as in the Zinfandel grape is the same variety as Primitivo, the constituent variety in this Puglian wine. It's a big sweet but tannic redcurrant and marzipan food red (spicy barbecues) with 14.5% alcohol.

NEW ZEALAND

🍷 9 **Waikato River Pinot Noir 2012** £7.99

Pale ruby colour is turning burnt-orange, nose of sour cherries and somehow peachstone, flavour is earthy soft-summer-fruit plump and silky; a fascinating and friendly Kiwi Pinot at a good price.

🍷 9 **Huntaway Central Otago Pinot Noir 2013** £9.99

Grown-up oaked and very firm slinky sour-cherry Pinot of some hauteur, though with a rich sweet note at heart, to go with a roast duck. Price is very fair for this sort of quality.

ROMANIA

🍷 8 **Surprisingly Good Pinot Noir 2014** £4.99

'Surprisingly' (in the name) because it's Romanian? Brightly healthy proper Pinot summer-red-fruit nose and flavour with a crisp lemon edge; entirely legitimate.

SOUTH AFRICA

🍷 8 **Morrisons Cabernet Sauvignon 2014** £4.49

Ripe but restrained recognisable Cabernet of healthy blackcurrant hue is 'sensational with steak' says the label. With respect, I suggest sausages.

🍷 8 **Morrisons Pinotage 2014** £4.49

Spicy-tarry savour in the right Pinotage tradition is healthy and toothsome and good value; 14% alcohol.

RED WINES

S. AFRICA

🍷 8 **M Signature South African Shiraz 2014**　£6.99
There's a seductive spicy-pruny ripeness amid the dark tannic fruit of this butch Swartland heavyweight; long flavours, lasting healthy aftertaste; 14.5% alcohol.

SPAIN

🍷 8 **Montelciego Rioja Joven 2013**　£4.49
Young ('joven') and unoaked pure Tempranillo, cheery with cassis fruit and healthily plump; picnic red at a good price.

🍷 8 **The Duke 2013**　£7.99
I do hope the rise in wines with silly names doesn't turn into a flood, but I like this dotty blend of Tempranillo with small measures of Shiraz, Garnacha and Merlot by Rioja bodega Muriel. It's oaked, sweetly cassis ripe with a nice tannic grip, and decidely Spanish.

🍷 8 **Bodegas Borsao Tres Picos 2013**　£14.99
Pure Garnacha from Aragon – a big smooth mélange of blackberry-spice-plum flavours in mellow unison made, amazingly, without any oak contact; my note compares it mysteriously with Châteauneuf du Pape. Online only.

PINK WINES

FRANCE

🍷 8 **Les Richoises Syrah Rosé 2014** £4.99
Pale coral, dry, fresh Mediterranean pink at a sensible price.

🍷 8 **Cellier des Princes Rosé 2013** £6.99
From the Rhône, mostly Grenache, it's ripe, firmly fruity and unusually dry-finishing.

ITALY

🍷 8 **Luisella Bardolino 2013** £4.99
Salmon-coloured, sour-cherry nose, redcurrant and cherry light dry fresh fruit; pink Veronese wine with some character.

WHITE WINES

ARGENTINA

🍷 8 **M Signature Torrontes 2014** £6.99
From Argentina's national white grape variety, known for its muscat-grapey style, this is true to form with extra tang, probably contributed by the 10% Sauvignon Blanc added to the mix.

AUSTRALIA

🍷 8 **M Signature Adelaide Hills Chardonnay 2013** £9.99
Happily balanced, near-elegant McGuigan wine delivering exuberant fruit, comforting oak and reviving freshness.

AUSTRIA

🍷 8 **M Signature Grüner Veltliner 2014** £6.99
Pungency and spice in the background to a clean, fresh rendering of this exotic dry food wine; nuanced and refreshingly characterful.

WHITE WINES

Morrisons

CHILE

9 Casillero del Diablo Chardonnay 2014   £7.99
Universal wine from Concha y Toro but whenever I come across anything under this brand I can't help taking notice; this is a healthy coconutty vivid apple-fresh, creamily seductive and thoroughly delightful all-rounder.

8 Cono Sur Reserva Riesling 2014   £8.99
Full, ripe and rich Riesling of leesy apple essence with a style all its own that I must call 'dry'. Very likeable and Rieslingophiles should not hold back. Online only.

FRANCE

8 La Sablette Muscadet 2014   £4.99
By the standards of this AC's often fiercely green wines this is a pussy-cat, relatively soft and gentle in its briny saline fruit, but it's not flabby and will please the more-cautious palate.

8 M Signature Touraine Sauvignon Blanc 2014   £6.99
Boldly bright and green Loire pure varietal with a good spate of refreshing lush fruit.

8 Bordeaux Sauvignon Blanc 2014   £7.99
Healthy green-grass pure varietal in the restrained Bordeaux style has lift and tang.

8 M Signature Pinot Gris 2013   £7.99
Smoky, exotic Alsace off-dry aperitif wine has well-managed sweetness and a fine poise.

WHITE WINES

🍷 8 **Paul Mas Clairette 2014**   £7.99
Paul Mas's Languedoc wines proliferate in every
supermarket but here at least is one I haven't seen
elsewhere, from the Clairette grape, a variety much used
for vermouth and sparkling wine. This is a ripe-tasting
dry still white that put me in mind of both Chardonnay
and Chenin Blanc. I liked it.

🍷 8 **Première Vouvray 2014**   £8.49
This balanced Chenin Blanc from the picturesque Loire
Valley appellation has eager crisp orchard fruit and honey
richness in an artful balance; fine aperitif and a match for
creamy-sauce dishes too; 11.5% alcohol.

🍷 8 **M Signature Petit Chablis 2014**   £8.99
Leesy-minty, mineral and by no means 'small' Chablis by
reliable La Chablisienne co-operative; an authentic treat.

🍷 10 **M Signature Chablis Premier Cru 2012**   £14.99
Just one-tenth of the must for this luscious wine was
fermented in oak barrels but there is a clear – and
delectable – vanilla richness imparted to the classic leesy-
mineral-steely fruit; finishes with a tangy but not abrupt
lemon acidity. Top Chablis at an inevitable price, but for
the right occasion, not to be missed.

🍷 8 **Italian White**   £3.99
Non-vintage dry pure Trebbiano from the Abruzzo has
wholesome orchard fruit, a lick of blanched almond
richness and tastes Italian. The price seals the deal.

WHITE WINES

ITALY

🍷 8 **M Signature Fiano 2014** £5.49
Sweet almondy middle flavour to this perky and quite
crisp orchard-fruit dry wine from dependable Settesoli
co-op of Sicily is satisfying and good value.

🍷 8 **M Signature Verdicchio 2014** £5.49
Sherbet lemon nose, quite brisk with brassica-fresh green
nutty fruit and a very little residual sweetness.

NEW ZEALAND

🍷 8 **Waikato River Sauvignon Blanc 2014** £6.99
Bracing Marlborough grassy-green refresher includes a
mysterious one-eighth part of Chardonnay; still liked it,
especially at the price.

🍷 9 **M Signature Marlborough Sauvignon Blanc
2014** £8.49
Exciting gooseberry zest jumps out of the glass with the
first sniff of this cracker, made by starry Yealands Estate,
rushing on to eager grassy-nettly green depths of classic
Kiwi flavour, finishing with snappy uplift.

PORTUGAL

🍷 7 **Morrisons Vinho Verde** £4.49
Inexpensive non-vintage very gently prickly number
self-described as 'crisp and fresh' but is quite sweet with
retained sugar and just 8.5% alcohol.

🍷 8 **M Signature White Douro 2014** £7.99
There's not much white wine made in the Douro Valley,
Port being the main concern, but here's a fine mélange
of flavours from dried apricot to marzipan and crunchy
brassica all incorporated into a dry and quite inspiring
whole.

WHITE WINES

SOUTH AFRICA

🍷 8 **Morrisons Chenin Blanc 2015** £4.49
Bargain dry aperitif with plenty of reassuring peachy-apricot fruit

🍷 8 **Morrisons Sauvignon Blanc 2015** £4.49
Fresh and citrussy' says the label on this bright new Western Cape pure varietal, and it does not lie. Good value.

🍷 8 **M Signature Chenin Blanc 2014** £6.99
Well-made ripe Swartland wine shows artful balance between honeyed fruit (with a little oak contact here) and fresh crispness; nice partner for Asian fish dishes.

🍷 8 **Kalander White 2014** £7.99
Chenin-Blanc-led Swartland blend is fresh and nuanced with a lick of toffee richness; food wine – white meats as well as assertive fish dishes.

SPAIN

🍷 8 **M Signature Albariño 2013** £7.99
Galician speciality showing correct sea-breeze freshness, cabbage whiteness and a lick of blanched nut richness.

SPARKLING WINES

8 M Signature Champagne Brut   £18.99
Easy creamy crowd-pleaser by Louis Kremer for those
who don't like their champagne too green.

FORTIFIED WINES

9 M Signature Palo Cortado Sherry 37.5cl   £5.99
Rare and beautiful sherry by top bodega Lustau has
glowing amber colour, wildly fruity-nutty perfume and
pungent, preserved-fruit, nutty rich flavours all in the
context of a 'dry' sherry; 19% alcohol. From a fine in-
house range of sherries, all of which should be served
chilled.

Sainsbury's

Sophie Hogg, head wine buyer at Sainsbury's, admits to being 'in relentless pursuit of producing best in class, affordable own brand wines'. She means it. Her three own-label tiers, respectively the House, Winemakers' Selection and Taste the Difference ranges, are now at the very centre of Sainsbury's wine offering.

Two-thirds of the wines in the following pages come from those ranges, and include some of the top buys this year. In fairness, the laurels are shared with some excellent branded wines. Besides awarding maximum points to four in-house wines, I have similarly lauded perennial Loire red Domaine du Colombier Chinon for a fabulous 2012 vintage.

One of my top scores goes to a sherry, Winemakers' Selection Amontillado, at just £5.50 for a full-size 75cl bottle. It tasted quite miraculously good to me and the price is incomprehensible. This is one of several new (or at least 'repackaged') own-label sherries from two great bodegas, Lustau and Williams & Humbert, introduced by Sainsbury's this year. I've tasted a number of them and have been astounded. Maybe, just maybe, Sainsbury's will succeed in their commendable mission to turn customers on to the world's best aperitif wines.

Promotions in the stores continue as before. As well as discounting individual wines on a monthly basis,

Sainsbury's regularly offers a week-long blanket 25 per cent off the whole lot for purchases of six or more bottles, bringing individual-promo wines down to very low prices indeed.

RED WINES

ARGENTINA

🍷 9 Winemakers' Selection Malbec 2014 £5.00
Deep, inky purple colour and dark, savoury, muscular juiciness give this top-value Mendoza varietal (with 15% Syrah) real force and charm. Great with barbecues and chilli dishes.

🍷 8 Taste the Difference Fairtrade Morador Malbec 2014 £8.00
Nicely tensed dark, spicy and gripping meaty red from Argentina's flagship grape made in Tolkienian mountain country at Fairtrade Bodega Casa del Rey; 14% alcohol.

AUSTRALIA

🍷 8 Taste the Difference Chateau Tanunda Barossa Cabernet Merlot 2013 £10.00
This mellow monster (14.5% alcohol) brimming with sweet-briar ripeness is discreetly supported by oak contact; nicely set up.

CHILE

🍷 9 Taste the Difference Chilean Pinot Noir 2013 £8.00
Light-touch Aconcagua wine by Errazuriz, pale and enticingly perfumed, nicely anticipating the long, sweetly ripe and limpid strawberry-raspberry fruit; slinky and balanced.

🍷 8 Taste the Difference Curicó Valley Chilean Merlot 2013 £8.00
Chilean Merlot is its own act, and here's a good one, deep purple, poised between exuberant black-cherry plushness and brisk brightness with a clean edge.

RED WINES

FRANCE

8 **SO Organic Shiraz Vin de Pays d'Oc 2014**   £6.00
It's Syrah at home in France, not Shiraz, but I have no other quibble with this ecologically correct Beziers red; sinewy, spicy and appropriately wholesome.

8 **Winemakers' Selection Vin de Pays d'Oc Merlot 2014**   £6.00
Purple Mediterranean party glugger with juicy blueberry highlights and a good grip.

10 **Domaine du Colombier Chinon 2012**   £7.00
Utterly consistent Loire red from Cabernet Franc grapes, the embodiment of leafy redcurrant crunchy freshness, a wholly unique red-wine style that seems cheap for the thrills it delivers. At the tasting Malcolm Gluck told me he actually buys this wine. He likes it that much. Me too.

9 **Taste the Difference Côtes du Rhône Villages 2013**   £7.00
Crunchy-juicy Chapoutier-made red of wholesome appeal with proper Côtes du Rhône spice and verve, has an enticing ruby-purple colour and ideal weight, long on briary fruit and a great match for starchy foods as well as meats; 14% alcohol.

8 **La Patrie Côtes de Bordeaux 2014**   £7.00
I am shamefully prone to stepping past anything from the Bordeaux hinternland, but this Merlot from Castillon merits a stop. It's young, vigorous, cassis ripe and generous, and well-made.

RED WINES

**9 Taste the Difference Languedoc Rouge
2014** £8.00
Yet another solid vintage for this big (14% alcohol), dark,
garrigue-spiced winter red by Mediterranean all-rounder
Jean Paul Mas.

8 Les Champs Clos Sancerre 2013 £12.00
Red Sancerre is made entirely from Pinot Noir grapes and
this one plainly so. Pale, limpid pigeon's eye colour, fresh
strawberry-raspberry perfume, pure defined Pinot fruit is
edgy and elegant; dare to try a little chilled; a fine and
costly extravagance.

9 Moulin-à-Vent Château des Jacques 2010 £16.00
Mature Beaujolais cru from an individual estate owned
by giant Louis Jadot is expensive but irresistible: every
inch the juicy, vivid rush-of-fruit Beaujolais style but
complex, long and grippy with balancing tannin. Special.

8 Château Cambon La Pelouse 2011 £20.00
From the heart of the Médoc close to Margaux, this is an
aspiring claret. You get deep ruby colour already showing
a tinge of browning and a rich, coffee-cedar-leather luxury
aroma en route to a silky and well-developed plummy-
black fruit. From the 'Fine Wine' selection it delivers a lot
for the premium price, which is not always to be counted
on at around this mark.

**8 Winemakers' Selection Montepulciano
d'Abruzzo** £6.00
Bouncy-briar non-vintage fun red with a crafty lick of
oak at a sensible price.

FRANCE

ITALY

RED WINES

Sainsbury's (vertical, left margin)

ITALY

🍷 **10** Taste the Difference Barbaresco 2012 £10.00
This is a young wine, but part-matured in new oak casks and already showing orange in the limpid ruby colour. It is such an artful contrivance, with sweet nuttiness and cherry richness on the nose and slinky, gently gripping summer-ripe berry fruit. Barbaresco is among Italy's flagship wines and this is an authentic introduction to the style; 14% alcohol.

PORTUGAL

🍷 **9** Winemakers' Selection Portuguese Red £5.00
Largely from Port grapes, this has a corresponding deep-purple colour, spicy black-fruit nose and fruit contained by a gentle grip of tannin. Convincingly Portuguese and jolly cheap.

S. AFRICA

🍷 **8** Winemakers' Selection South African
Shiraz Cabernet 2014 £6.00
May I suggest that this comes across as a French style of wine rather than a Cape one? Plump and ripe but restrained and balanced, instantly likeable blend with 14.5% alcohol and an appealing price.

SPAIN

🍷 **8** Sainsbury's House Tempranillo £4.50
This bright and brambly party red from the grape of Rioja, grown far away from home in south-east Spain is healthy and juicy.

🍷 **8** Winemakers' Selection Old Vine Garnacha
2013 £6.00
Sourced from 40-year-old vines in 'the north of Spain' this geographically uncertain varietal is entirely positive in its gutsy, intense, nicely stalky-edged black-fruit fullness; a lot of wine for the money.

RED WINES

8 **Castillo de Albai Rioja Tinto 2014** £6.50
Cheery blackcurranty pure Tempranillo is unoaked and
untypical, I'd say, of Rioja (except for the gaudy label)
but likeable in its own juicy way.

9 **Era Costana Rioja Crianza 2012** £7.00
Now this really is a Rioja, if unusually opaque in colour,
with a big smoky-oaky nose, vanilla-spice-cassis fruit and
a keen price.

9 **Taste the Difference Cepa Alegro Rioja
Reserva 2009** £10.00
Colour's browning in this sweet and creamy new-oak
luxury reserva; the fruit is defined and juicy and cuts
convincingly through the richness in nifty balance;
already rounded and supple but has years ahead of it.

8 **Condado de Haza Ribera del Duero
Crianza 2011** £17.00
Massive deep-coloured pure Tempranillo from rightly
revered region with intense mulberry-plum-blackcurrant
(you name it) rich fruit encased in puckering tannin
which surely needs time to integrate; fabulous wine in
early development; 14.5% alcohol.

SPAIN

PINK WINES

FRANCE

🍷 **8** **Winemakers' Selection Côtes du Rhône Rosé
2014** £6.00
Tastes fresh and pinkly pink and is reasonably priced. Job
done.

🍷 **8** **Taste the Difference Bordeaux Rosé** £8.00
Salmon-pink mainly Merlot wine from Blaye has a trim
Bordeaux character.

🍷 **7** **Les Caillottes Sancerre Rosé 2014** £13.00
Pure Pinot coral-pink luxury item from the famed
Loire appellation is brisk and defined with an authentic
strawberry Pinot streak. Expensive.

GERMANY

🍷 **8** **Winemakers' Selection Rheinhessen
Dornfelder Rosé** £5.00
Dornfelder is Germany's own black-grape variety, created
to make home-grown reds; seems a pity to divert it to
pink wine but this magenta blackcurrant-juice number
has a quirky charm of its own. Sweet but finishes quite
dry, and cheap.

S. AFRICA

🍷 **8** **L'Avenir Rosé de Pinotage 2015** £8.00
Very newly made shell-pink Western Cape wine has a
centred sunny strawberry fruitiness of purity and lively
freshness; stands out.

WHITE WINES

AUSTRALIA

🍷 8　**Yalumba Y Series Viognier 2014**　　　£10.00
Mellow yellow apricotty varietal from famed Barossa winery; stands out for brightness as well as distinctive ripeness.

FRANCE

🍷 8　**Winemakers' Selection Sauvignon
　　　Colombard 2014**　　　£6.00
This artful refresher from the Gers has tang and balance.

🍷 8　**Taste the Difference Muscadet Sèvre et
　　　Maine sur Lie 2014**　　　£7.00
Crisp and briny rather than green and challenging, a pleasingly coloured, boldly fruity and extracted seafood matcher from the famed appellation in the Atlantic estuary of the Loire.

🍷 8　**Trésor de Loire Cuvée 845 Chenin Blanc
　　　2014**　　　£7.00
Very dry, verging on ascetic, for Chenin Blanc, but then you get a lift of richness in alluring contrast to the brassica brace; fascinating, refreshing, rare; 11.5% alcohol.

🍷 9　**Taste the Difference Languedoc Blanc 2014**　£8.00
Another terrific vintage for this self-effacingly named southern blend of Grenache Blanc, Marsanne, Vermentino and Viognier offers a delightful table of tropical-fruit flavours wrapped up in orchard-fruit freshness.

🍷 8　**Taste the Difference Mâcon Villages 2014**　　£8.00
From a considerable crowd of these wines this year, a standout sunshine ripe Chardonnay niftily balancing peach and brassica.

WHITE WINES

Sainsbury's *(vertical text, left margin)*

FRANCE

🍷 8 **Taste the Difference Petit Chablis 2014**   £9.00
Genuine article from a vanishing appellation; lush leesy Chardonnay in the inimitable Chablis manner.

🍷 10 **Taste the Difference Pouilly Fumé 2014**   £12.00
Stonking, richly-coloured prestige-appellation Loire Valley Sauvignon of surpassing mineral river-fresh lushness and complexity. World-class wine of which Sainsbury's should be proud (and no doubt is).

🍷 9 **Taste the Difference Sancerre 2014**   £13.00
Stony-fresh, lush, tangy and long Loire Sauvignon lives fully up to the exalted name of the appellation; best vintage of this perennial prizewinner I can remember.

GERMANY

🍷 9 **Winemakers' Selection Riesling 2013**   £5.00
Racy Rheinhessen has a lick or two of residual sweetness all within an artful balance; a fine introduction to simple Rhine Riesling at a giveaway price; 9% alcohol.

🍷 8 **Dr Loosen Graacher Himmelreich Riesling Kabinett 2014**   £13.00
Crisp, even prickly Moselle of vigorous freshness with a rush of crunchy apple Riesling fruit and lush underlying grapey sweetness; nicely poised if a little pricey; note just 7.5% alcohol.

ITALY

🍷 8 **Sainsbury's House Soave**   £4.00
Recognisable green-fruit style with a suggestion of nutty richness; easy and fresh with 11.5% alcohol.

WHITE WINES

🍷 8 **Taste the Difference Gavi 2014**   £8.00
Ubiquitous Piedmont dry white from ubiquitous
Piedmont wine giant Araldica; almond-rich on the nose
with contrasting crisp and bright focused white fruit;
11.5% alcohol.

🍷 8 **Taste the Difference Verdicchio Classico
dei Castelli di Jesi 2014**   £8.00
Ornate nomenclature and a naff amphora-style bottle
give this Ancona dry white an outdated message, but it's
a decent fresh and zingy wine with a trace of the green (as
in the grape name Verdicchio) in the colour that translates
into the tangy orchard flavour.

🍷 9 **Taste the Difference Greco di Tufo 2013**   £10.00
This handsomely packaged Campania dry white from
volcanic terrain is rich in colour with aromas and flavours
evoking everything from apple to apricot, from fennel to
sage. Great food white – from creamy pasta to grilled fish
to roast chicken.

🍷 8 **Mount Riley Marlborough Sauvignon Blanc
2014**   £8.00
Liked this one (new to me) best among Sainsbury's Kiwi
Sauvignons: crisp, green, grassy and lush.

🍷 8 **Cloudy Bay Chardonnay 2013**   £20.00
There's always a frisson with Cloudy Bay: yellow colour,
suitably plush aromas and plenty of toffee-apple and
chilled white peach plumpness in fine balance; 14%
alcohol.

ITALY

NEW ZEALAND

WHITE WINES

PORTUGAL

🍷 8 **Winemakers' Selection Vinho Verde**   £5.00
Non-vintage but lively and fairly interesting, fairly sweet
green wine at a fair price.

S. AFRICA

🍷 9 **Zalze Reserve Chenin Blanc 2013**   £10.00
Clever mix of sweetly ripe orchard fruit and seaside
freshness in what is blindingly obviously the work of a
master winemaker – which it is; Cape Chenin at its best,
one of the world's more underrated wine styles; 14%
alcohol.

SPAIN

🍷 8 **Castillo de Albai Rioja Blanco 2014**   £7.00
Modern (ie not oxidised) white Rioja, unoaked but with
lots of lush, even rich, appley fruit; a very attractive
example of a wine style in short supply.

🍷 8 **Taste the Difference Viñedos Barrihuelo**
Rioja Blanco 2014   £8.00
And here's another white Rioja already, sweet-nosed but
niftily balanced and fresh in the modern style.

Sainsbury's

SPARKLING WINES

 Winemakers' Selection Champagne
Blanc de Noirs Brut   £20.00

Made from six parts Pinot Meunier and four parts Pinot Noir this consistent perennial has a big bakery perfume, mellow, long fruit and a confidence-fostering fullness and brightness about it. I cannot fault it, and substantial discounts regularly reduce the shelf price, itself down to £20 from £22.25 last year. It has been drafted into the Winemakers' Selection range this year, with no diminution of appeal.

Winemakers' Selection Champagne
Blanc de Blancs Brut   £20.00

I have long preferred the more-nuanced Blanc de Noirs counterpart of this fine all-Chardonnay fizz but this year am a shade equivocal. This seems to have acquired an extra allure of complexity, maturity and creaminess of late and it has won some prestigious prizes. Lovely wine that may soon challenge my sense of loyalty.

Winemakers' Selection Champagne Rosé
Brut   £23.00

Attractive shell-pink colour is reflected in the fresh touch-of-strawberry pink fruit, very dry and crisp but tasting developed and balanced; Chardonnay coloured with a measure of Pinot Noir, this is a bit of a star in the bewildering firmament of fashionable pink fizz.

FRANCE

FORTIFIED WINES

10 **Winemakers' Selection A Blend of Amontillado Medium Dry Sherry** £5.50

Beautiful, glowing bronze-gold colour, perfume of toasty hazelnuts and smoky-raisiny pungency lead into flavours of pure fruit-and-freshness. An ineffably good dry sherry of instant appeal to be drunk well chilled. The price, for a full-size bottle, is incomprehensible; 17% alcohol.

9 **Winemakers' Selection Dry Manzanilla Superior Sherry** £5.50

The name's a bit of a mouthful but so is this fantastically fresh, tiggerishly tangy and briny speciality pale-as-white, bone-dry aperitif wine, made to be served very cold in a decent-sized glass. It is unbelievably cheap for the quality; 15% alcohol.

9 **Taste the Difference Fino Sherry 50cl** £8.00

Seriously pungent, white-nutty, lemon-tangy intensely flavoursome and arch-refreshing drink-it-ice-cold pale dry sherry by legendary bodega Lustau; 15% alcohol.

9 **Taste the Difference 12-Year-Old Oloroso Sherry 50cl** £8.00

Bronze in colour and with a divine toasty preserved fruit aroma ('oloroso' means fragrant), this is dry but rich and pungent mature sherry of dimension, burgeoning with flavours evoking roasted nuts and figs and other very good things; 20% alcohol.

SPAIN

Sainsbury's

Tesco

They're soldiering on at Tesco. Writing anything constructive about the stricken giant might appear out of step, but I must nevertheless report that numerous Tesco wines I've lately tasted suggest this particular department of the ailing enterprise appears to be in rude health.

There, I've said it. I can also report that at the huge tasting held for the press in London early in 2015, in the eye of the media storm, the Tesco wine team were in their usual good spirits. Nick Hood, quality manager, very kindly sought me out to say how much he and his colleagues appreciated what I had written about Tesco wine in last year's edition of this book.

It's a pleasure. But changes are taking place. The wine range is definitely being thinned out. Quite a few old favourites of mine have been delisted. I guess it simplifies matters, saves money. On the other hand, there are new wines and new vintages of established regulars to recommend, with wines from the basic 'Tesco Simply' range to the flagship 'Finest' tier (now numbering more than a hundred) featuring conspicuously.

As ever, the wines are promoted and discounted with almost fevered regularity. What never fails to surprise me is that many of those cut in price are from the own-label ranges as well as the mass-market brands. Given that the Finest wines are pretty sensibly priced in the first place, you can see where the real bargains are. And just like at Sainsbury's, 25-per-cent-off everything offers are regularly applied on top.

Discounts are generally replicated online at Tesco's dedicated wine website. The site is always worth a browse for other offers as well, particularly for internet-only 'fine' (as distinct from Finest) wines being sold off at bargain prices, perhaps to replenish the troubled behemoth's waning fortunes.

RED WINES

ARGENTINA

9 **Finest Argentinean Malbec 2014**   £7.99
Attractively packaged supple but grippy oaked pure
Malbec by ace winery Catena; has spicy savour to match
highly flavoured meat dishes. It grows on you.

8 **Palo Marcado Old Vines Malbec 2012**   £12.99
Grand wine aged two years in new oak casks, this is a
darkly opaque plush-velvet monster (14.5% alcohol)
nevertheless showing defined mulberry-blueberry Malbec
flavours. A conversation piece from the Upper Calchaqui
Valley, one of the world's highest vineyard regions.

AUSTRALIA

8 **Sister's Run Barossa Grenache 2012**   £8.00
A chance to retaste this well-liked discovery from a year
past; it's a pale-coloured but firmly fruity raspberry-
blackberry compote of juiciness with 14.5% alcohol.
Online by the case only.

9 **Terra Rossa Cabernet Sauvignon**
Parker Estate 2006   £21.49
Its brown hue makes this Coonawarra monster look like
an oloroso sherry in the glass, but the wild blackcurrant
aromas and silky cassis fruit, by no means overwhelmed
by the creaminess of the oak contact, suggest something
more akin to an old and blue-blooded claret; outrageously
expensive – £128.94 by the case online only – and a
stonking 15% alcohol, but I loved it.

8 **St Hallett Old Block Shiraz 2010**   £32.00
Dare I say an Aussie icon? A straight, gorgeous, Barossa
wine for a grand occasion at a pertinent price of £192 per
six-bottle case, online only. The point is that it lives up to
its reputation.

RED WINES

Tesco

CHILE

9 Vineyards Merlot   £3.99
Chilean Merlot can have a sunny ripeness all its own, and this vintage blend delivers it – a big kiss of bold black-cherry fruit, nicely balanced and wholesome. Bargain.

8 Finest Kulapelli Cabernet Sauvignon 2014   £7.99
Hardy perennial, regularly discounted, has a new-look label but it's still brimming with ripe briary flavours; a healthy unoaked food red in the pure-fruit Chilean tradition.

8 Finest Cuartel Merlot 2013   £8.99
This was aged in French new oak barrels, an extravagant indulgence at the price. It's certainly toasty, but the fruit comes richly through and the acidity's keen. Made by dependable Montes winery.

8 Finest Las Lomas Shiraz 2013   £8.99
Creamy blend with Cabernet and Carmenere holds together well in a package of bramble and blackcurrant ripeness; a winter warmer with a touch of class.

9 Terrunyo Carmenere 2011   £18.00
For special occasions – Christmas dinner comes to mind – a dense, spicy and silkily luxuriant rendering of the Carmenere, as grown in Concha y Toro's most-prized vineyards. This is a flagship wine, a clear statement that Chile can compete with the very best worldwide; as such, it's keen value at £108 for a six-bottle case online; 14.7% alcohol.

RED WINES

FRANCE

7 Simply Claret £4.15
The price is the most interesting element here; it's lean but not mean and does resemble the red Bordeaux style, as it should from the dependable merchant-producer Yvon Mau.

9 Tesco Beaujolais £4.49
Particularly perky purple juice bomb from the 2014 vintage – a surprise success after a bad start – this is proper bouncing young Beaujolais, bright, juicy and brisk, and alluringly priced. Serve gently chilled.

9 La Folie Douce Pinot Noir 2013 £4.99
La Folie Douce is an exciting new brand designed to appeal to younger drinkers in an easy-to-drink style', it says here. I liked it anyway for its full colour (for Pinot), bloomy strawberry nose and grippy-brisk summer-red-fruit fleshiness; proper Pinot of unstated French origin. Don't be put off by the cheesy cafe-style label.

8 Tesco Vintage Claret 2013 £4.99
Substantial Merlot-Cabernet blend 'sourced from all over the Bordeaux region' according to maker Yvon Mau; has centred wholesome fruit and an easy grip of tannin.

10 Finest Fitou Domaine D'Aubermesnil 2013 £5.99
I relish the chance to recork a wine and then reopen it three days later to see how it does. This one, if anything, had improved on its dark, savoury-spicy typically briary Languedoc fruit, with a lick of toffee ripeness at the intense core of the flavour. A marvel, and I believe the back-label advice that it 'will age for another five years with careful cellaring'. Stock up.

FRANCE

8 Tesco Beaujolais Villages 2014   £6.49
Pleasing juicy red tastes as if made from Pinot Noir rather
than Gamay grapes, as Beaujolais is supposed to be.
Liked it just the same.

10 Finest Côtes Catalanes Grenache 2014   £6.99
This has been such a favourite of mine for so long that
I can hardly bear to report that the 2014 might be the
last vintage. So snap it up now – it's an intense brambly
food red from Perpignan, full of wholesome, nourishing
spicy flavours. The price has been £7.49 for years but
the present £6.99 is itself regularly discounted. The
stablemate Carignan, another perennial top buy, has
already been dropped.

9 Finest St Chinian 2013   £8.99
This was a new launch in 2014, and a welcome one,
appealingly crimson in colour and perfumed in the
authentic fruits-of-the-forest style of this distinctive
Mediterranean hill-country appellation. I like the back-
label pointer to 'dark, balsamic aromas'. Brambly and
juicy with pleasing tannic abrasion, it's been cunningly
enriched with some oak-finished wine in the blend.

7 Finest Crozes Hermitage 2013   £9.99
I liked this northern Rhône staple; the price is not
scandalous and it has the right silky Syrah intensity and
grip. But it needs time.

RED WINES

8 **Château Fonguillon Montagne
St Emilion 2012** £10.49

Deep-purple violet-plum-perfumed proper St Emilion
satellite claret, already slinky with cherry-cassis rounded
dark fruit and clean-finishing; class act that will repay
decanting.

7 **Château de Pena Côtes du Roussillon 2013**£10.99

A clear candidate for discounting, this dark, ripe and
peppery meat-matcher is in the authentic Roussillon style;
14% alcohol.

9 **St Joseph Cuvée D'Automne 2012** £14.99

St Joseph, neighbour to the Northern Rhône's famous
Hermitage ACs, makes some sublime reds from Syrah
and this whimsically named co-operative effort illustrates
the style: gamey, gently spicy and darkly silky with prune
and blackberry notes; I daresay it even has an autumnal
ripeness. Liked it even at full price, and even better on
discount at £7.50. Be vigilant.

9 **Château Sénéjac 2010** £15.00

Tesco.com is still stuck with a vast array of expensive
2009 classed-growth clarets (Lafite at £800 a bottle,
anyone?), so to buy into the subsequent vintage might
appear foolhardy. But the 2010s are just as good, and a
lot better value (Lafite a mere £700, I see), especially at
cru bourgeois level, where most of Tesco's 2010s reside.
This is a dark, intense, velvety Haut Médoc of good name
with juicy and roasty-toasty Cabernet-led fruit, already
drinking well. Online by the case only.

FRANCE

RED WINES

FRANCE

8 **Gigondas Domaine Des Bosquets 2010** £20.00
This deep, concentrated, gamey-spicy Rhône icon from a stellar vintage is already rich, rounded and wickedly sumptuous; guaranteed to please, which it should, at twenty quid a bottle – online only by the six-bottle case; 15% alcohol.

ITALY

8 **Tesco Sicilian Red** £4.19
Earth, spice and moorland savour, it says in my note. A typically baked and sunny island red from Sicily's own Nero d'Avola grape blended with Syrah into a substantial pasta-pizza red at a giveaway price.

7 **Tesco Valpolicella** £5.49
Pale colour just north of rosé and a perky cherry perfume lead into a juicy-crunchy refreshing fruit flattered by chilling; good of its kind and 11% alcohol.

9 **Finest Teroldego 2013** £7.99
From the Alto Adige region of northernmost Italy, a ripe but edgy blackberry food red of real character with minty, leafy highlights in the long, succulent flavour. Made by Cavit, a giant co-op making two-thirds of all the region's wines including many of the best of them.

8 **Finest Nero d'Avola 2014** £7.99
From giant Sicilian co-op Settesoli, a major Tesco supplier, a sweet-briar-smelling dark and spicy red-meat wine with plummy depths and plenty of grunt.

RED WINES

7 Finest Chianti Riserva 2012 £8.99

Big Sangiovese (excepting mysterious 5% Cabernet Sauvignon) from Chianti giant Piccini is ripe, rounded and recognisable; regularly discounted – the full price is fanciful.

9 Finest Barolo 2011 £14.99

After years of waiting for a good vintage of this Tesco annual, along come two in succession. This is a worthy follow-up to the sleek 2010 (look out for any still on shelf), a lovely mellow wine in terms of its easing ruby colour, affecting tar-and-roses perfume and silky but grippy roasty-pungent summer-sweet red fruit; 14% alcohol.

9 Finest Amarone 2012 £29.99

The price makes the inclusion of this fabulous wine an academic exercise, but I do commend it to the irresponsibly rich or reckless. Made by great Valpolicella outfit Allegrini, you get a dense, blood-red appearance, coffee and spiritousness on the nose and a huge, smooth, black-fruit body of flavour with the uniquely abrading amarone ('bitter') texture that gives this rare wine its exciting balance between opulence and austerity; 15.5% alcohol.

8 Brancott Estate Terroir Series Pinot Noir 2013 £15.00

Awatere Valley (Marlborough) vineyards of giant Brancott (French-owned producer of half New Zealand's wine) makes this pale but intense cabbagey Pinot in exalted style; it's a long, elegant safe bet at a price, online only at £90 per six-bottle case.

ITALY

NEW ZEALAND

RED WINES

PORTUGAL

 Finest Douro 2013 £6.00
Best vintage so far for this persistently underpriced table
wine from the Douro Valley, home of Port. You get the
spicy blackberry whiff familiar from the fortified wines,
deep colour and generous darkly ripe fruit with plenty
of grip.

SOUTH AFRICA

 Simply Pinotage £4.49
Signature entry-level wine shows off the tarry, spicy,
minty Pinotage style to good effect.

Finest Swartland Pinotage 2014 £6.99
Whopping big smoothie has been enriched with oak
contact but the dark, mulberry, plummy-spicy fruit shines
bright; a great match for highly seasoned meat dishes;
14.5% alcohol.

SPAIN

La Nonna Rioja Joven 2013 £4.29
New introduction emblazoned with a fluorescent orange
label is almost as bright as it looks – and just as cheap.
Vigorous blackcurranty recognisable drink-it-now (joven
means young) unoaked Rioja both friendly and juicy;
mellow rather than callow.

La Nonna Rioja Crianza 2010 £4.99
Same lurid packaging as its youthful stablemate, above,
but this one's colour is browning gently with age and
offering a sweet-briar and vanilla nose as an introduction
to the rounded, if lightweight, authentic Rioja savour.
Good value.

RED WINES

8 Finest Viña Mara Rioja Reserva 2010   £9.49
SPAIN Likeable blackcurrant-pie-with-cream bloom from this
dark and muscular modern Rioja by Baron de Ley.

PINK WINES

9 Finest Domaine de Sours Rosé 2014   £6.79
An own-label bottling (I've just noticed) from a famous
Libourne (Bordeaux right bank) estate, this is a keen-
edged Merlot-based blend with glowing colour, briar fruit
and delicate poise; really rather good value.

7 Finest Grenache Rosé 2014   £7.99
Party-frock pink from Languedoc is full of fruit, very dry
and fresh for summer food matches.

8 Finest Sancerre Rosé 2013   £9.99
Delicate salmon colour and soft-summer-fruit style to this
ritzy Pinot Noir pink; fresh and fun and arguably worth
the premium price.

8 Finest Nero d'Avola Rosé 2014   £5.99
Very pale Sicilian wine with plenty of artfully balanced
ripe-fresh, pink-tasting brambly fruit. Nice fish match.

9 Simply Portuguese Rosé   £3.99
In its Mateus-shaped bottle, I anticipated the very faintly
spritzy style but liked the pale magenta colour and softly
but not overtly sweetly beguiling fruit, from a mix of
grape varieties common to Port production, but of
unstated location; likeable novelty, very cheap and just
10.5% alcohol.

PINK WINES

8 **Simply Garnacha Rosé** £4.69
Generous in magenta colour, briary fruit and brisk, dry
freshness; a proper pink-tasting bargain from Aragon;
why pay more?

SPAIN

WHITE WINES

8 **Finest Argentina Torrontes 2014** £6.99
Muscat nose to the fore in this dry but generously fruity
example from Argentina's indigenous white grape, made
by ace winery Catena. To suit well-seasoned fish and
poultry dishes.

ARGENTINA

9 **Finest Denman Semillon 2013** £8.99
Proper fruit-salad pong of pineapple and peach, even
banana and grape, comes off this exotic Hunter Valley dry,
fresh and exceedingly distinctive varietal. It's complicated
but simply delicious, just 10% alcohol and you should try
it as a lively aperitif or with salad-based dishes.

9 **Tim Adams Clare Valley Semillon 2011** £10.49
Golden in colour and with a delectable diesel note on
the peachy-citrus nose, this new-oak fermented dry-but-
luscious and contemplative, succulent sipper is delicious
already and will live for years.

AUSTRALIA

9 **Tim Adams Clare Valley Riesling 2013** £10.79
Perpetually dependable and strongly distinctive limey-
racy rush-of-flavour dry wine is a citrus extravaganza
featuring grapefruit aromas and lemon acidity; 11.4%
alcohol.

WHITE WINES

AUSTRALIA

♈ 10 McGuigan The Shortlist Chardonnay 2011 £15.00
I gave this wine a top score last year and Tesco is still
listing it at the same price per case online. So here it
is again: a luscious, de-luxe, new-oak fermented and
beautifully balanced Adelaide Hills pure varietal of great
character.

♈ 8 Lateral Pinot Grigio 2014   £4.49
It includes 15% Sauvignon Blanc, which maybe adds the
zest to a serviceable PG offering more interest than Italian
counterparts, which are never this cheap; 11.5% alcohol.

CHILE

♈ 8 Finest Piwen Chardonnay 2014   £7.99
My notes on this witter on about pineapple and peach
on the nose, then coconut and toffee in the fruit – that'll
be the oak contact some of the wine had in the cellars of
the estimable Ventisquero winery, in Chile's Casablanca
region, whence it comes. A nicely constructed pure
Chardonnay of broad charm.

**♈ 8 Finest Campo Lindo Organic Sauvignon Blanc
2014   £8.99**
From big but bio-conscious producer Cono Sur, an
asparagus-scented, grassy-tangy refresher of intriguing
complexity. Sold in only 20 stores, so it might be a long
search.

FRANCE

♈ 9 Simply Muscadet   £4.49
Non-vintage but from the 2014 harvest ('weather
conditions were warm and dry' Tesco reports) a crisp,
tangy and briny but not eye-watering mussel-matcher
from the famed Loire estuary appellation at a snip of a
price, which I've seen reduced to a barking £3.37 in one
multibuy offer.

WHITE WINES

🍷 9 **Tesco Côtes de Gascogne Blanc 2014** £4.69
Tellingly tangy and citrussy seaside-fresh dry wine by dependable Gascon co-op Plaimont has unstinting white fruit and a modest 11% alcohol. Bargain.

🍷 9 **Lucien Marcel Vin de Pays du Gers Blanc 2013** £4.79
The vineyards of Gers in Gascony mostly supply the wine-wash for Armagnac brandy, but here's a dry white with its own considerable merits. It's a proper fruit salad of lush, layered, long and fresh flavours of real charm at a risible price and just 11.5% alcohol.

🍷 10 **Tesco Anjou Blanc 2014** £4.99
Maybe it's just me, but Chenin Blanc from the Loire Valley seems out of this world these days. This one from the 'dream' 2014 vintage is crisply dry but with plumpness of body, honey notes and plenty of whoomph; there's nothing quite like it and yet it's a versatile wine for aperitif drinking and food matching. Ridiculously cheap, and just 11% alcohol.

🍷 7 **La Folie Douce Sauvignon Blanc 2014** £4.99
Jazzily packaged new vin de France brand is recognisably warm-weather Sauvignon in the softer style for the cautious palate.

🍷 9 **Tesco Vouvray 2014** £5.99
From the same source (Lacheteau winery) as the Anjou above, a plush, fleshy Chenin Blanc miraculously poised between dry, lemony freshness and honeyed richness; 11% alcohol.

WHITE WINES

🍷 8 Tesco Mâcon Villages 2014 £6.79

Attractive lemon-gold colour, apple-blossom perfume and spring-fresh Chardonnay fruit from Burgundy's southern outpost. Authentic.

🍷 9 Finest Vin de Pays Gascogne Gros Manseng Sauvignon Blanc 2014 £7.99

Perennial Gascon favourite delivers a lively combination of lush Manseng fruit brisked up with keen, nettly Sauvignon by Bordeaux winemaker cheerily named Pascal Poussevin. Special, and frequently discounted.

🍷 9 Tesco White Burgundy 2014 £7.99

This luscious unoaked sunnily ripe Mâcon Chardonnay by ubiquitous Blason de Bourgogne is a benchmark wine. Curious to know what decent white burgundy tastes like? Try this one.

🍷 8 Finest Alsace Gewürztraminer 2013 £7.99

I am a great believer in Alsace Gewürztraminer, even though the everyday ones can be oversweet. This one has 10 grammes of residual sugar, but is nicely balanced with dry spiciness, lychee perfume and other good Gewürz trademarks.

🍷 9 Tesco Finest Chablis 2013 £9.99

The best vintage yet for this one: bright balance of flinty typical green-gold Chablis fruit and a nifty twang of lemon at the edge.

WHITE WINES

France

🍷 8 **Grand Conseillier Chardonnay 2013**   £11.99
From Bouchard Aîné, a leading producer-merchant in Burgundy, this is an intriguingly balanced Midi 'Vin de France' with sherbet and citrus zest aligned to sweet-apple, creamy burgundy-style Chardonnay fruit. Artful and convincing at the discounted price I paid, £5.99. At full price, it is less appealing.

🍷 8 **Finest Chablis Premier Cru 2011**   £13.99
You pay for the name Chablis, and with this one it's worth the outlay. Authentically rich-mineral Chardonnay flavours enhanced by some oak-matured wine in the blend, all from well-rated vineyards made by omnipresent Blason de Bourgogne.

🍷 8 **Finest Meursault 2013**   £20.99
Lovely plump Chardonnay from famed Côte de Beaune AC, licky-rich from new-oak contact and mineral-elegant in the grand white burgundy manner; lives up to expectations and will repay the investment.

GERMANY

🍷 8 **Simply Riesling**   £4.79
Grapey-sweet, not sugary, Rhine non-vintage Riesling has balancing apple crispness and 10.5% alcohol.

🍷 8 **Finest Steillage Riesling 2014**   £7.99
Bold apple fruit with raciness and zest in this robust Mosel will make it a satisfying match for Asian menus as well as a fine aperitif; 11% alcohol.

WHITE WINES

8 Peter & Peter Riesling Mosel 2014   £7.99
Peter Griebeler, winemaker for Zimmermann Graeff &
Müller of Zell, producers of Tesco's own-label German
wines, gets the double name-check on this austere,
fermented-out (11.5% alcohol) dry, apple-crisp and
mineral pure Riesling. Nice match for charcuterie.

9 Simply Soave   £4.79
Made by Cantina di Soave, established 1898 and 'one of
Italy's most prestigious and innovative wine producers'
(says Tesco) this non-vintage (but 2014 harvest) Verona
classic is stunningly good at what seems a needlessly
nugatory price. For a start, it tastes like Soave, with
green freshness, healthy tangy fruit and fleeting blanched-
almond savour.

9 Finest Fiano 2014   £5.49
Forgive me if I have misreported the price, which
prevailed at the time I tasted the wine. The 2013 vintage
cost £7.99 and this is its equal. A robustly fruity varietal
by Sicilian giant Cantine Settesoli (where I once spent
a hugely educational and jolly day), it combines a rush
of crunchiness with a lick of nutty, even honeyed sunny
ripeness.

8 Finest Gavi 2014   £7.99
Attractive new vintage of this Piedmont dry-but-exotic
food white has lashings of crisp orchard fruit balanced by
a crafty richness imparted through the addition of late-
harvested, extra-ripe grapes (all Cortese, the constituent
variety) to the must.

WHITE WINES

8 Finest Pecorino 2013   £7.99
This Abruzzo refresher has focused, eager orchard fruit with plenty of interest.

8 Finest Marlborough Sauvignon Blanc 2014 £7.49
Gooseberries and grass in breezy profusion in this well-priced refresher by admired Yealands Estate.

7 Tesco Vinho Verde   £4.29
This non-vintage wine is from the 2014 vintage, says Tesco, perplexingly. It's pale, faintly spritzy, delicately sweet but fresh and just 9% alcohol. Jolly cheap, too.

8 Falua Arinto Reserva 2012   £12.50
I assumed this gold-coloured, pineapple-perfumed, richly flavoured dry white must be from Chardonnay until learning from the name that it's entirely from Arinto grapes cultivated in the baking Lisbon zone of Bucelas, a near-extinct DOC that clearly warrants renewed attention. Luscious oak-fermented lobster white (Christmas turkey, too). Online by the six-bottle case only.

10 Simply Chenin Blanc   £4.49
I have to award maximum points because this delightful aperitif wine is faultlessly good and incontestible value. You get a genteel honey whiff en route to the fresh, dry, peachy fruit and clean, citrus-trimmed finish. Chenin is the white-wine grape to watch. Those grown for this wine came from the Olifants River Valley of the Western Cape.

WHITE WINES

S. AFRICA

🍷 9　**Finest Swartland Chenin Blanc 2014**　£6.99
Cracking new vintage of a perennial favourite, this is
beautifully balanced between the poles of peachy lushness
and twangy crispness for which the Chenin grape is
rightly celebrated; 14% alcohol.

SPAIN

🍷 8　**Viña Pomal Blanco 2013**　£10.00
White Rioja is scarce, and here's a good one worth
seeking out – though online only by the six-bottle case. It's
fermented partly in new oak casks and has recognisable
creamy vanilla richness, but it's a modern-style wine
really, not at all oxidised and bright with sweet-apple
lushness.

SPARKLING WINES

FRANCE

🍷 9　**Finest 1531 Blanquette de Limoux 2012**　£10.99
Well-coloured, eagerly bubbly fizz from an under-
appreciated Languedoc AC has peach and banana notes
on the nose and generous fruit, finishing briskly clean;
from local Mauzac grapes plus a dash of oak-fermented
Chardonnay. The number 1531 refers to the date 'the first
sparkling wine in the world was produced by the monks
of the Saint Hilaire abbey' in Limoux. Amazing.

🍷 9　**Finest Premier Cru Champagne Brut**　£19.99
Very attractive and consistent Chardonnay-dominated
blend from prestige vineyards with plenty of colour,
biscuity aroma and lasting, mature-tasting flavours;
frequently discounted.

SPARKLING WINES

🍷 **10** **Finest Grand Cru Vintage Champagne
Brut 2007** £24.99
Rich colour and brioche nose give great allure to this
maturing Chardonnay from top-rated vineyards; the
2007 vintage is evidently selling slowly – this is its third
year on shelf, and time is doing it no disservice.

🍷 **8** **Chanoine Frères Vintage Champagne 2009** £29.99
This bright, lemony but mellow and yeasty vintage is
really delicious, but not worth the full price; at the time
of tasting it was on offer at £15 – a bargain.

🍷 **7** **Borgo Molino Motivo Prosecco Brut** £15.00
Premium price Prosecco from Treviso is a clear step up
from the ordinary; discreetly honeyed crisp-pear fruit and
persistent sparkle; 11% alcohol. Online by the case only.

Waitrose

The Waitrose juggernaut rumbles on. The John Lewis grocer might have been overtaken this year in terms of sales by upstart foreign discounter Aldi, but Waitrose's share of the overall market increased just the same, to 5.1 per cent. More interesting in the present context is the figure for wine sales. Waitrose now has 7.7 per cent of the take-home market – half as much again as its operation overall (if my maths is right).

Tasting the wines, you can see why. There are about a thousand of them, and the number is not padded out with dross. Until really quite recently, own-label wines have accounted for a tiny proportion of the whole, but I see that of the 80-odd products I have singled out here, one in four is an in-house wine.

I am particularly taken with the range from Bordeaux, starting with Good Ordinary Claret 2014, one of my bargain wines of the year. Bordeaux had tricky vintages from 2011–2013 but 2014 was blessed by weeks of perfect sunshine in the ripening season right up to picking, so there are some joyful 'ordinary' reds to be found. Waitrose's Bordeaux offerings range back much further of course, and if there is a time and a place to rediscover claret at sensible prices (forget the rip-off classed-growths) it's now, at Waitrose.

Other strengths include the marvellous range of in-house sherries, which I have failed to mention among my notes this year but always heartily recommend, and the bargain own-label range that includes Waitrose Mellow and Fruity Spanish Red at £4.99, awarded maximum points because it is exactly what it claims to be and is a proper bargain.

A relatively new facility is the Waitrose Cellar online wine service. There has for many years been a good wine website but this is now integrated with the stores via a 'Click and Collect' service. You can order any six bottles up to 9pm online for collection from 2pm the next day in more than 300 of the stores. Or, as before, you can simply have the wine – any mix, any quantity – delivered to you at home.

RED WINES

ARGENTINA

🍷 8 **Tilimuqui Single Vineyard Fairtrade Organic Cabernet Sauvignon/Bonarda 2014** £7.99
The elaborate label name seems to say it all, but I will add that this right-on Famatina Valley red has vigorous raspy roasty-ripe fruit and will nicely accompany game pie.

🍷 8 **Norton Winemaker's Reserve Malbec 2012** £10.99
Macho roasted-fruit slinky-savoury and gripping food red (meat, meat, meat) might be too much for delicate tastes but a great comfort in a mean midwinter; 14.5% alcohol.

🍷 9 **Waitrose Soft and Juicy Chilean Red 2014** £4.99
The jolly dark purple colour, foretold by the label, is matched for perkiness by the lively defined berry fruit of this Merlot-Cabernet blend; every inch a Chilean party red and terrific value.

🍷 8 **Waitrose Reserva Carmenère 2014** £7.99
The pleasing purple colour might be carmine, the esoteric hue that gives the Carmenère grape its name. Other merits include a wholesome hedgerow-fruit ripeness, slinky texture and clean finish; 14% alcohol.

🍷 8 **Luis Felipe Edwards Bin Series Merlot 2014** £8.99
Chocolate-cherry charm of well-controlled sweetness makes this an immediately appealing easy-drinking oaked red full of life.

CHILE

RED WINES

10 Good Ordinary Claret 2014 £5.19
From the Bordeaux boondocks maybe, but this is an out-and-out bargain. Remarkably ripe Merlot-led blend is deep in ruby colour, blackberry-bushy-tailed on the nose and generous in fleshy dark fruit with a nice breakfast tea tug of tannin at the finish. Good claret. Nothing ordinary about it.

8 Fitou Mme Claude Parmentier 2013 £7.99
Revived 1980s brand by Languedoc's Val d'Arbieu is a welcome reminder of the diminished Fitou appellation: spicy dark and generous sausage red.

8 Blason du Rhône Côtes du Rhône-Villages 2013 £8.99
Grippy, gently peppery Grenache-dominated blend with brightly defined fruit and wholesome ripeness; 14% alcohol.

8 Paul Mas Grenache/Syrah Vin de Pays d'Oc 2014 £8.99
Smoothly wrought blend by ubiquitous producer has lifted black briary fruits and creamy oak with silk and spice.

9 Les Complices de Loire Les Graviers Chinon 2013 £10.00
Excitingly juicy pure Cabernet Franc from the Loire has just the right leafy, stalky greenness lifting the wild redcurrant fruit; don't be afraid to chill this crunchily delicious red to bring out the freshness.

FRANCE

RED WINES

FRANCE

9 Crozes-Hermitage Les Hauts de Pavières
   2012   £11.49

Pure Syrah from the Cave de Tain, which makes 60% of all Crozes-Hermitage and seems to know what it's doing, has a lovely plummy nose and tense black fruit slung in velvet oak richness all with a spicy savour; in short, a special wine of its kind, and at unusually rational price for this appellation.

8 Domaine de la Croix de Chaintres
   Saumur-Champigny 2014   £12.79

Deep-purple lipsmacking Loire Cabernet Franc by local winemaking dynasty Filliatreau is eagerly young and fresh but with a seductive richness.

9 Château Liversan 2011   £13.49

Ooh, lovely pliant athletic dark and ripe Haut-Médoc from an even blend of Merlot and Cabernets has plumpness as well as power and well-developed tannic structure; classic 'Cru Bourgeois' claret at a sensible price to drink now.

8 Domaine Paul Blanck Pinot Noir 2013   £14.99

Rare Alsace red, austere by Pinot measures but strongly expressive of the grape's elusive cherry-soft-summer-fruit characteristics; a fine wine for Pinot fanciers, at a price.

8 Château Fonréaud 2011   £15.99

Beguiling Cabernet-Sauvignon/Merlot from the Listrac commune of Bordeaux's Haut-Médoc, nicely evolved with intense but mellow blackberry fruit and damson twang; a class act for drinking or keeping.

RED WINES

8 **Chorey-lès-Beaune Domaine Maillard**
Père et Fils 2013 £16.99
No other supermarket dabbles in Burgundies like this: sweetly inviting pure Pinot, sleekly oaked and already mellow and earthily seductive; online only.

9 **Domaine Chante-Alouette-Cormeil 2001** £19.99
A St Emilion Grand Cru in dignified maturity, this retains a very deep colour now just browning at the edge, and a dark, gamey-cedary black-fruit aroma of a very inviting kind; it's sleek, rich and developed in fruit and drinking perfectly now; the price is absolutely fair.

9 **Château Laroque 2009** £28.99
Another (see Domaine Chante-Alouette-Cormeil above) St Emilion Grand Cru, this time from an epic harvest now coming round nicely. Colour borders on liquorice and the rich perfume gives a clue to the 87% Merlot in the blend, banging with black-cherry intensity; the fruit, robed in creamy oak (much of it new) is lavishly intense but seductive rather than daunting and the 15% alcohol is worn comfortably.

9 **Tsantali Organic Cabernet Sauvignon 2013** £9.49
Deep crimson-purple pure varietal from Macedonian resort of Halkidiki has slick blackcurrant depths made lush with vanilla oak; I would never guess its Greek provenance but that doesn't deprive it of distinctive and likeable character; 14% alcohol.

8 **Il Venti Rossi 2014** £4.49
Quirky mix of Sangiovese, Merlot and Montepulciano grapes from Emilia-Romagna has vivid dark berry fruits, a nifty cutting acidity and easy charm; spaghetti red.

FRANCE

GREECE

ITALY

Waitrose

RED WINES

8 Castel Boglione Barbera/Cabernet Sauvignon 2013 £5.99
Novel blend of 20% Cabernet by Piedmont producer Araldica has dark blackberry-pie savour with proper nutskin-dry edge to the fruit; a nice juicy pasta matcher.

9 Valpolicella Cantina di Soave 2014 £6.49
Proper cherry and almond kernel lightweight with a nice raspberry whiff and crisp finish; 11.5% alcohol.

8 Torre del Falco Nero di Troia 2013 £7.99
The label catches your eye and the wine, from Bari in Puglia, does not disappoint with its tight dark and spicy black fruits, satisfying weight and roasty grip.

9 Malvirà Nebbiolo delle Langhe 2012 £11.99
Alluring translucent colour in this elusive Piedmont wine is already browning and the fine bitter-cherry and rose-bloom perfume speaks of much costlier Barolo; sleek, silky and satisfying.

8 Waitrose Ripasso di Valpolicella Classico Superiore 2012 £11.99
Lots of centred, pruny, dark-chocolate, amarone-bitter elements to the slicky oaked fruit in this lush Veronese speciality red; 14% alcohol.

8 Terre da Vino Barolo Riserva 2004 £22.99
Magnificent mature example of Italy's premier red wine has limpid ruby colour orange at the rim and an enthralling nose of violets and roses, bitter cherry and liquor; fruit is silky, pure and intense with a firm tannic grip; on offer at £17.99 at time of writing, a bit of a bargain if it's repeated.

ITALY

RED WINES

N. ZEALAND

8 **The Ned Pinot Noir 2013** £14.99
Pale but intense and ripe with firm tannin grip, you get a lot of plump, round soft-summer-fruit and nicely defined acidity for the money; 14% alcohol.

PORTUGAL

8 Tinto da Anfora 2013 £9.99
Enduring second wine of great Quinta Bacalhôa in the Alentejo is stygian-dark and properly Portuguese in its clovey-minty spiciness and briary savour; grippy with tannin but already relishable; 14.5% alcohol.

8 Waitrose Douro Valley Reserva 2012 £10.99
Made at redoubtable Quinta de Rosa, it has a porty perfume and just the sort of midnight-dark, minty and concentrated black-fruit flavours you'd expect from these vineyards; 14.5% alcohol.

ROMANIA

8 Waitrose Romanian Pinot Noir 2014 £6.99
Pale, raspberry-ripple style party Pinot to drink cool; not sweet, nicely balanced.

S. AFRICA

8 Boekenhoutskloof The Chocolate Block
2013 £20.99
Intrigued? It's a soupy Syrah-based blend with dark damson depths, silky texture and a fair old grip of spicy tannin; no chocolate to speak of, but it's wholesomely rich and concentrated; 14.5% alcohol.

RED WINES

10 **Waitrose Mellow and Fruity Spanish Red**
2014 **£4.99**
I gave the 2013 vintage a top score for value last year
and must repeat it: soft but defined pure Garnacha from
Campo de Borja near Rioja of reliable vigour and, yes,
mellowness.

9 **Ribera del Duero Bodegas Buena Allende**
La Vega 2011 **£9.99**
Rich, minty, exotic, dark, intense pure-Tempranillo
Duero classic evoking those chocolate-covered prunes
from Poland; distinctive maturing oaked wine of terrific
character at an unusually fair price for this fashionable
zone.

8 **The Cubist Old Vine Garnacha 2013** **£9.99**
Perennial Waitrose speciality with a fancy new name, this
has brightly red fruit of bracing, sinewy, spicy vitality;
very intense and ripe and 14.5% alcohol. It has a fancy
new 'cork' too – the 'world's first zero carbon footprint
wine closure' from 'renewable, plant-based materials
derived from sugar cane'. So now you know.

8 **Waitrose Viña Lorea Rioja Crianza 2011** **£9.99**
Juicily ripe, vanilla-enriched middleweight Rioja of easy
charm.

8 **Lafou El Sender 2013** **£11.49**
Perplexing blend of Garnacha with Syrah from Catalan
DO Terra Alta is comparable to a Rhône red from
the same grape mix, only deeper and denser with lush
creaminess (some new oak) and vivid spice; 14% alcohol.
Roast venison would be a match.

SPAIN

RED WINES

USA

8 **Waitrose Californian Cabernet Sauvignon**
2013 £6.49
Cheerfully sweet but brightly clean blackcurrant everyday
glugger has a toffee hint all from natural ripeness, as no
oak; it grows on you.

8 **Fog Head Reserve Pinot Noir 2013** £14.99
From Monterey, California, a Burgundian-style
raspberries-and-cream rendering of the Pinot with poise
and ripeness.

PINK WINES

FRANCE

8 **Cuvée Fleur Rosé 2014** £4.99
From Cinsault grapes grown near Béziers, a pale petal
pink just short of dry with delicate summer-fruit flavours,
unfussily fresh and cheap.

8 **Waitrose Provence Rosé 2014** £8.49
Very pale salmon colour and briskly dry, but plenty of
pink-tasting summer-fruit (mainly Grenache) with lively
freshness.

ITALY

8 **Vignale Pinot Grigio Rosé Blush 2014** £6.29
Sounds a fright, but this Veneto pink does at least taste
like Pinot Grigio and gets its blush from the pink skins
left on the must; the flavour has a trace of cassis.

SPAIN

8 **Waitrose Ripe and Juicy Spanish Rosé 2014** £4.99
Stablemate to the excellent red, a pale-magenta, brisk and
dry Garnacha with briary fruit.

PINK WINES

SPAIN

 8 Muga Rioja Rosado 2014 £9.99

Best pink tried at Waitrose, but not cheap, it has a nice orange-pink glow and positive crisp defined strawberry-fresh fruit.

WHITE WINES

ARGENTINA

8 Tilimuqui Single Vineyard Fairtrade Organic Torrontes 2014 £7.99

A new style to me, crisp Torrontes of concentrated intensity in which the Muscatty character of this indigenous Argentine variety translates into an exotic but poised and palpably dry, fresh effect.

AUSTRALIA

 8 d'Arenberg The Hermit Crab Viognier/ Marsanne 2013 £10.99

Old favourite of undiminished appeal in this exotic, fruit-salad and grassy-fresh new vintage; a versatile food wine to match everything from prawn cocktail to roast pork.

AUSTRIA

 8 Waitrose Grüner Veltliner 2014 £7.99

Distinctive fruit-blossom-perfumed, gently pungent dry aromatic food white with notes of sage and thyme (I might be imagining this) both exotic and fresh.

CHILE

8 Waitrose Vibrant and Grassy Chilean White 2014 £4.99

Sauvignon supported by Chardonnay make up the mix in this does-what-it-says-on-the-tin own label, bottled in the UK to help keep the price down.

WHITE WINES

🍷 **7** **Bolney Estate Autumn Spice 2014** £10.99
Exotic aromatic smoky-dry Sussex wine from Müller-Thurgau and Reichensteiner grapes; 11.5% alcohol.

🍷 **10** **Hen Pecked Picpoul de Pinet 2014** £7.99
The western Med's new favourite dry white has become fashionable and here's a cash-in brand (hen-pecked/picpoul – geddit?) with a cross-looking chook on the label. But it happens to be a brilliant wine: crackingly (geddit?) fresh and tangy with masses of green-white fruit flavours. Huge fun.

🍷 **9** **Fief-Guérin Muscadet Sur Lie 2014** £7.99
Scintillating bone-dry sea-fresh mussel-matcher from outré Côtes de Grandlieu zone of the famed Loire estuary appellation; masses of lush green briny fruit with a citrus edge.

🍷 **8** **Le Grand Ballon Sauvignon Blanc 2014** £8.49
Tangy green Loire pure varietal has an alluring trace of sweetness amid the refreshingly direct grassy fruit.

🍷 **9** **Waitrose White Burgundy 2014** £8.99
Pure Mâconnais Chardy lush and with plenty of crisp apple liveliness; it takes a lot to make an individual wine stand out from the southern-Burgundy crowd, and this one has it.

🍷 **9** **Saint-Véran Vignerons des Grandes Vignes 2014** £9.99
I found, I swear, banana as well as peach on the nose of this slurpy Mâconnais gem; lavish unoaked Chardonnay is sweetly ripe and mineral bright, a lovely balance.

WHITE WINES

**⚏ 8 Cave de Beblenheim Kleinfels Riesling
2013** £10.49
Characteristic Alsace dry Riesling has a lemony perfume
with an agreeable petrol note and generous apple-limey
rush of fruit. Well made by a chap called Patrick le Bast'rd.

⚏ 8 Vouvray Château de Montfort 2014 £11.99
Lush Loire Chenin Blanc is brilliantly balanced between
zing and honey to create a white wine at once nourishing
and refreshing; 11.5% alcohol. A fine aperitif but a match
too for Asian menus, poultry, creamy pasta and more.

⚏ 9 Waitrose Sancerre La Franchotte 2014 £14.99
Such is the consistency of quality even in generic Loire
Sauvignon these days that the premium payable for
Sancerre can seem unwarrantable, but this one is worth
it. Flinty but richly extracted river-fresh grassy fruit is
uplifting and memorable.

⚏ 9 Waitrose Sauternes 2009 37.5cl £16.99
Ravishingly delicious dessert wine from top Sauternes
estate Château Suduiraut is yellow gold with an inspiring
honeysuckle-toffee-tang-of-citrus nose and ambrosial-
toasty but delicately trim finish; 14% alcohol. Special.

⚏ 8 Josmeyer le Fromenteau Pinot Gris 2010 £23.99
From one of Alsace's top names, a luxuriantly ripe but
steely and smoky aperitif/dessert wine; 14% alcohol.
Made according to biodynamic principles.

WHITE WINES

FRANCE

🍷 8 **Joseph Drouhin Puligny-Montrachet 1er Cru Les Folatières 2012** £55.00
Thank you, Waitrose, for a taste of this sumptuous white burgundy, gold in colour, butter-rich in peachy perfume and all creamy apple-pie and glittering minerality in the mouth. If you can afford a wine like this, be assured you'll get your money's worth.

GERMANY

🍷 8 **Leitz Rüdesheimer Magdalenenkreuz Riesling Kabinett 2014** £13.99
Delicate Rhine wine has fine floral perfume, racy apple crispness and mineral vivacity with grapey-honey background; 10% alcohol.

ITALY

🍷 8 **Cantina di Soave 2014** £5.29
No flannel (it's not a 'classico' or a 'superiore') but it has a nice gold-green colour, brisk lemon and blanched almond nose and fresh crisp white, typical Soave fruit; 11.5% alcohol.

🍷 8 **Waitrose Soave Classico 2014** £6.99
Cool summer breezes blowing down the Alpine foothills of the Dolomites give warm days and cool nights' to the vineyards where they grow the Garganega grapes for this, says Waitrose. Sip this pleasing brassica-fresh, crisp green, fleetingly nutty dry wine and imagine it all.

🍷 8 **Cantina Gadoro Fiano 2014** £7.99
From starry Beneventano zone of the Campania a plump, even honeyed, spin on the popular Fiano theme, with vivid orchard fruit, quite dry, nicely balanced; fine aperitif.

WHITE WINES

ITALY

Y 8 **Rocca Murer Sauvignon Blanc 2014**   £8.99
Given the quality of Sauvignon from the Loire and New
Zealand, who'd buy it from the Trentino? This sub-
Alpine item has in its favour a cool freshness that could
evoke mountain air, a greengage twang to the eager fruit
and a fleeting ripe grapiness that defy its Italian-ness.

Y 8 **LaVis Storie di Vite Pinot Grigio 2014**   £9.75
Consistently above-average Italian PG has a sweet pear
nose, soft but balanced mouth-filling white orchard fruits
and a hint of smokiness.

NEW ZEALAND

Y 8 **Cowrie Bay Sauvignon Blanc 2014**   £7.49
Likeable asparagus pong and tangy green, even piquant
nettly fruit in this value refresher.

Y 8 **Mud House Sauvignon Blanc 2014**   £9.99
This one sings: vivaciously zesty and grassy Wairau,
Marlborough, pure varietal that thrills and stimulates.

Y 8 **The Ned Pinot Grigio 2014**   £9.99
It still has that teeny pink tinge, which tells you the rosy-
skinned PG grapes have had a good steeping and, I like
to think, helps give this brilliantly named Waihopai River
wine its unique exotic, smoky, refreshing and uplifting
appeal.

Y 8 **Huntaway Reserve Chardonnay 2012**   £10.99
It seems to me there's not always much point to Kiwi
Chardonnay, but here's an interesting one: nutty, creamy
apple-pie style with New Zealand's own uniquely
glittering lively uplift.

WHITE WINES

PORTUGAL

8 **Quinta de Azeveda Vinho Verde 2014** £8.29
Ubiquitous brand by giant Sogrape has a definite tingle
and pleasing bristly white fruit that might just be a little
less-sweetened than before; 10.5% alcohol.

S. AFRICA

9 **Springfield Estate Special Cuvée**
Sauvignon Blanc 2014 £11.99
I'll say it's special – a super-ripe but also super-fresh
asparagus and sea grass thriller that puts even Kiwi
counterparts firmly in the shade.

8 **Waitrose Aromatic and Citrus Spanish**
Dry White 2014 £4.99
The apple-and-pear aromatics are upfront, the citrus
right at the end; bright, brisk refresher.

8 **Waitrose Libra Verdejo 2014** £7.49
From the Rueda region – always a good sign – a tangy,
seaside breezy dry wine with plenty of colour and a nifty
balance between white fruit and citrus acidity.

SPAIN

9 **Palacio de Fefiñanes Albariño 2014** £15.99
From Galicia's seaside DO of Rias Baixas, a fancy-
looking package with a brilliant lemon-gold colour,
gorgeous grassy nose and lashings of wild green fruit in
the very best Albariño tradition; top example of this now-
ubiquitous and trendy wine justifies the premium price.

USA

8 **Waitrose Californian Chardonnay 2013** £6.49
Proverbial sunshine in a glass, plumply, peachily ripe with
sweet-apple fruit but free of oak and all at a keen price.

SPARKLING WINES

8 **Crémant de Limoux Cuvée Royale Brut**   **£11.49**
Lively 70% Chardonnay blend with Pinot Noir and, oddly, Chenin Blanc, is fresh but creamily appealing with bready aroma and long flavours.

9 **Waitrose Champagne Blanc de Blancs
Brut**   **£24.99**
Yeasty-creamy long-fruited lush champagne gives a distinct impression of long bottle-age.

9 **Taittinger Comtes de Champagne
Blanc de Blancs Brut 2005**   **£100.00**
I had not tasted this de luxe champagne in years, but am now reminded it is a lot more than a mere bling brand; rich in colour, heavenly bakery nose, lush thrillingly nuanced tiny-bubble flow of flavours.

7 **Waitrose Prosecco**   **£7.49**
Quite fizzy, quite dry, quite good, quite cheap.

—*Making the most of it*—

There has always been a lot of nonsense talked about the correct ways to serve wine. Red wine, we are told, should be opened and allowed to 'breathe' before pouring. White wine should be chilled. Wine doesn't go with soup, tomatoes or chocolate. You know the sort of thing.

It would all be simply laughable except that these daft conventions do make so many potential wine lovers nervous about the simple ritual of opening a bottle and sharing it around. Here is a short and opinionated guide to the received wisdom.

Breathing

Simply uncorking a wine for an hour or two before you serve it will make absolutely no difference to the way it tastes. However, if you wish to warm up an icy bottle of red by placing it near (never on) a radiator or fire, do remove the cork first. As the wine warms, even very slightly, it gives off gas, which will spoil the flavour if it cannot escape.

Chambré-ing

One of the more florid terms in the wine vocabulary. The idea is that red wine should be at the same temperature as the room (chambre) you're going to drink it in. In fairness, it makes sense – although the term harks back to the days when the only people who drank wine were those who could afford to keep it in the freezing cold vaulted cellars beneath their houses. The ridiculously high temperatures to which some homes are raised by central heating systems today are really far too warm for wine. But presumably those who live in such circumstances do so out of choice, and will prefer their wine to be similarly overheated.

Chilling

Drink your white wine as cold as you like. It's certainly true that good whites are at their best at a cool rather than at an icy temperature, but cheap and characterless wines can be improved immeasurably if they are cold enough – the anaesthetising effect of the temperature removes all sense of taste. Pay no attention to notions that red wine should not be served cool. There are plenty of lightweight reds that will respond very well to an hour in the fridge.

Corked wine

Wine trade surveys reveal that far too many bottles are in no fit state to be sold. The villain is very often cited as the cork. Cut from the bark of cork-oak trees cultivated for the purpose in Portugal and Spain, these natural stoppers have done sterling service for 200 years, but now face a crisis of confidence among wine producers. A diseased or damaged cork can make the wine taste stale because air has penetrated, or musty-mushroomy due to TCA, an infection of the raw material. These faults in wine, known as 'corked' or 'corky', should be immediately obvious, even in the humblest bottle, so you should return the bottle to the supplier and demand a refund.

Today, more and more wine producers are opting to close their bottles with polymer bungs. Some are designed to resemble the 'real thing' while others come in a rather disorienting range of colours – including black. While these things can be a pain to extract, there seems to be no evidence they do any harm to the wine. Don't 'lay down' bottles closed with polymer. The potential effects of years of contact with the plastic are yet to be scientifically established.

The same goes for screwcaps. These do have the merit of obviating the struggle with the corkscrew, but prolonged contact of the plastic liner with the wine might not be a good idea.

Corkscrews

The best kind of corkscrew is the 'waiter's friend' type. It looks like a pen-knife, unfolding a 'worm' (the helix or screw) and a lever device which, after the worm has been driven into the cork (try to centre it) rests on the lip of the bottle and enables you to withdraw the cork with minimal effort. Some have two-stage lips to facilitate the task. These devices are cheaper and longer-lasting than any of the more elaborate types, and are equally effective at withdrawing polymer bungs – which can be hellishly difficult to unwind from Teflon-coated 'continuous' corkscrews like the Screwpull.

Decanting

There are two views on the merits of decanting wines. The prevailing one seems to be that it is pointless and even pretentious. The other is that it can make real improvements in the way a wine tastes and is definitely worth the trouble.

Scientists, not usually much exercised by the finer nuances of wine, will tell you that exposure to the air causes wine to 'oxidise' – take in oxygen molecules that will quite quickly initiate the process of turning wine into vinegar – and anyone who has tasted a 'morning-after' glass of wine will no doubt vouch for this.

But the fact that wine does oxidise is a genuine clue to the reality of the effects of exposure to air. Shut inside its bottle, a young wine is very much a live substance, jumping with natural, but mysterious, compounds that can cause all sorts of strange taste sensations. But by exposing the wine to air these effects are markedly reduced.

In wines that spend longer in the bottle, the influence of these factors diminishes, in a process called 'reduction'. In red wines, the hardness of tannin – the natural preservative imparted into wine from the grape skins – gradually reduces, just as the raw purple colour darkens to ruby and later to orangey-brown.

I believe there is less reason for decanting old wines than new, unless the old wine has thrown a deposit and needs carefully to be poured off it. And in some light-bodied wines, such as older Rioja, decanting is probably a bad idea because it can accelerate oxidation all too quickly.

As to actual experiments, I have carried out several of my own, with wines opened in advance or wines decanted compared to the same wines just opened and poured, and my own unscientific judgement is that big, young, alcoholic reds can certainly be improved by aeration.

Washing glasses

If your wine glasses are of any value to you, don't put them in the dishwasher. Over time, they'll craze from the heat of the water. And they will not emerge in the glitteringly pristine condition suggested by the pictures on some detergent packets. For genuinely perfect glasses that will stay that way, wash them in hot soapy water, rinse with clean, hot water and dry immediately with a glass cloth kept exclusively for this purpose. Sounds like fanaticism, but if you take your wine seriously, you'll see there is sense in it.

Keeping wine

How long can you keep an opened bottle of wine before it goes downhill? Not long. A re-corked bottle with just a glassful out of it should stay fresh until the day after, but if there is a lot of air inside the bottle, the wine will oxidise, turning progressively stale and sour. Wine 'saving' devices that allow you to withdraw the air from the bottle via a punctured, self-sealing rubber stopper are variably effective, but don't expect these to keep a wine fresh for more than a couple of re-openings. A crafty method of keeping a half-finished bottle is to decant it, via a funnel, into a clean half bottle and recork.

Storing wine

Supermarket labels always seem to advise that 'this wine should be consumed within one year of purchase'. I think this is a wheeze to persuade customers to drink it up quickly and come back for more. Many of the more robust red wines are likely to stay in good condition for much more than one year, and plenty will actually improve with age. On the other hand, it is a sensible axiom that inexpensive dry white wines are better the younger they are. If you do intend to store wines for longer than a few weeks, do pay heed to the conventional wisdom that bottles are best stored in low, stable temperatures, preferably in the dark. Bottles closed with conventional corks should be laid on their side lest the corks dry out for lack of contact with the wine. But one of the notable advantages of the new closures now proliferating is that if your wine comes with a polymer 'cork' or a screwcap, you can safely store it upright.

Wine and food

Wine is made to be drunk with food, but some wines go better with particular dishes than others. It is no coincidence that Italian wines, characterised by soft, cherry fruit and a clean, mouth-drying finish, go so well with the sticky delights of pasta.

But it's personal taste rather than national associations that should determine the choice of wine with food. And if you prefer a black-hearted Argentinian Malbec to a brambly Italian Barbera with your Bolognese, that's fine.

The conventions that have grown up around wine and food pairings do make some sense, just the same. I was thrilled to learn in the early days of my drinking career that sweet, dessert wines can go well with strong blue cheese. As I don't much like puddings, but love sweet wines, I was eager to test this match – and I'm here to tell you that it works very well indeed as the end-piece to a grand meal in which there is cheese as well as pud on offer.

Red wine and cheese are supposed to be a natural match, but I'm not so sure. Reds can taste awfully tinny with soft cheeses such as Brie and Camembert, and even worse with goat's cheese. A really extravagant, yellow Australian Chardonnay will make a better match. Hard cheeses such as Cheddar and the wonderful Old Amsterdam (top-of-the-market Gouda) are better with reds.

And then there's the delicate issue of fish. Red wine is supposed to be a no-no. This might well be true of grilled and wholly unadorned white fish, such as sole or a delicate dish of prawns, scallops or crab. But what about oven-roasted monkfish or a substantial winter-season fish pie? An edgy red will do very well indeed, and provide much comfort for those many among us who simply prefer to drink red wine with food, and white wine on its own.

It is very often the method by which dishes are prepared, rather than their core ingredients, that determines which wine will work best. To be didactic, I would always choose Beaujolais or summer-fruit-style reds such as those from Pinot Noir grapes to go with a simple roast chicken. But if the bird is cooked as coq au vin with a hefty wine sauce, I would plump for a much more assertive red.

Some sauces, it is alleged, will overwhelm all wines. Salsa and curry come to mind. I have carried out a number of experiments into this great issue of our time, in my capacity as consultant to a company that specialises in supplying wines to Asian restaurants. One discovery I have made is that forcefully fruity dry white wines with keen acidity can go very well indeed even with fairly incendiary dishes. Sauvignon Blanc with Madras? Give it a try!

I'm also convinced, however, that some red wines will stand up very well to a bit of heat. The marvellously robust reds of Argentina made from Malbec grapes are good partners to Mexican chilli-hot recipes and salsa dishes. The dry, tannic edge to these wines provides a good counterpoint to the inflammatory spices in the food.

Some foods are supposedly impossible to match with wine. Eggs and chocolate are among the prime offenders. And yet, legendary cook Elizabeth David's best-selling autobiography was entitled *An Omelette and a Glass of Wine*, and the affiliation between chocolates and champagne is an unbreakable one. Taste is, after all, that most personally governed of all senses. If your choice is a boiled egg washed down with a glass of claret, who is to dictate otherwise?

What wine
words mean

Wine labels are getting crowded. It's mostly thanks to the unending torrent of new regulation. Lately, for example, the European Union has decided that all wines sold within its borders must display a health warning: 'Contains Sulphites'. All wines are made with the aid of preparations containing sulphur to combat diseases in the vineyards and bacterial infections in the winery. You can't make wine without sulphur. Even 'organic' wines are made with it. But some people are sensitive to the traces of sulphur in some wines, so we must all be informed of the presence of this hazardous material.

That's the way it is. And it might not be long before some even sterner warnings will be added about another ingredient in wine. Alcohol is the new tobacco, as the regulators see it, and in the near future we can look forward to some stern admonishments about the effects of alcohol. In the meantime, the mandatory information on every label includes the quantity, alcoholic strength and country of origin, along with the name of the producer. The region will be specified, vaguely on wines from loosely regulated countries such as Australia, and precisely on wines from over-regulated countries such as France. Wines from 'classic' regions of Europe – Bordeaux, Chianti, Rioja and so on – are mostly labelled according to their location rather than their constituent grape varieties. If it says Sancerre, it's taken as read that you either know it's made with Sauvignon Blanc grapes, or don't care.

Wines from just about everywhere else make no such assumptions. If a New Zealand wine is made from Sauvignon Blanc grapes, you can be sure the label will say so. This does quite neatly represent the gulf between the two worlds of winemaking. In traditional European regions, it's the place, the vineyard, that mostly determines the character of the wines. The French call it *terroir*, to encapsulate not just the lie of the land and the soil conditions but the wild variations in the weather from year to year as well. The grapes are merely the medium through which the timeless mysteries of the deep earth are translated into the ineffable glories of the wine, adjusted annually according to the vagaries of climate, variable moods of the winemaker, and who knows what else.

In the less arcane vineyards of the New World, the grape is definitely king. In hot valleys such as the Barossa (South Australia) or the Maipo (Chile), climate is relatively predictable and the soil conditions are managed by irrigation. It's the fruit that counts, and the style of the wine is determined by the variety – soft, spicy Shiraz; peachy, yellow Chardonnay and so on.

The main purpose of this glossary is, consequently, to give short descriptions of the 'classic' wines, including the names of the grapes they are made from, and of the 70-odd distinct grape varieties that make most of the world's wines. As well as these very brief descriptions, I have included equally shortened summaries of the regions and appellations of the better-known wines, along with some of the local terms used to indicate style and alleged qualities.

Finally, I have tried to explain in simple and rational terms the peculiar words I use in trying to convey the characteristics of wines described. 'Delicious' might need no further qualification, but the likes of 'bouncy', 'green' and 'liquorous' probably do.

A

abboccato – Medium-dry white wine style. Italy, especially Orvieto.

AC – *See* Appellation d'Origine Contrôlée.

acidity – To be any good, every wine must have the right level of acidity. It gives wine the element of dryness or sharpness it needs to prevent cloying sweetness or dull wateriness. If there is too much acidity, wine tastes raw or acetic (vinegary). Winemakers strive to create balanced acidity – either by cleverly controlling the natural processes, or by adding sugar and acid to correct imbalances.

aftertaste – The flavour that lingers in the mouth after swallowing the wine.

Aglianico – Black grape variety of southern Italy. It has romantic associations. When the ancient Greeks first colonised Italy in the seventh century BC, it was with the prime purpose of planting it as a vineyard (the Greek name for Italy was *Oenotria* – land of cultivated vines). The name for the vines the Greeks brought with them was Ellenico (as in Hellas, Greece), from which Aglianico is the modern rendering. To return to the point, these ancient vines, especially in the arid volcanic landscapes of Basilicata and Cilento, produce excellent dark, earthy and highly distinctive wines. A name to look out for.

Agriculture biologique – On French wine labels, an indication that the wine has been made by organic methods.

Albariño – White grape variety of Spain that makes intriguingly perfumed fresh and spicy dry wines, especially in esteemed Rias Baixas region.

alcohol – The alcohol levels in wines are expressed in terms of alcohol by volume ('abv'), that is, the percentage of the volume of the wine that is common, or ethyl, alcohol. A typical wine at 12 per cent abv is thus 12 parts alcohol and, in effect, 88 parts fruit juice.

The question of how much alcohol we can drink without harming ourselves in the short or long term is an impossible one to answer, but there is more or less general agreement among scientists that small amounts of alcohol are good for us, even if the only evidence of this is actuarial – the fact that mortality statistics show teetotallers live significantly shorter lives than moderate drinkers. According to the Department of Health, there are 'safe limits' to the amount of alcohol we should drink weekly. These limits are measured in units of alcohol, with a small glass of wine taken to be one unit. Men are advised that 28 units a week is the most they can drink without risk to health, and for women (whose liver function differs from that of men because of metabolic distinctions) the figure is 21 units.

WHAT WINE WORDS MEAN

If you wish to measure your consumption closely, note that a standard 75 cl bottle of wine at 12 per cent alcohol contains 9 units. A bottle of German Moselle at 8 per cent alcohol has only 6 units, but a bottle of Australian Chardonnay at 14 per cent has 10.5.

Alentejo – Wine region of southern Portugal (immediately north of the Algarve), with a fast-improving reputation, especially for sappy, keen reds from local grape varieties including Aragones, Castelão and Trincadeira.

Almansa – DO winemaking region of Spain inland from Alicante, making great-value red wines.

Alsace – France's easternmost wine-producing region lies between the Vosges Mountains and the River Rhine, with Germany beyond. These conditions make for the production of some of the world's most delicious and fascinating white wines, always sold under the name of their constituent grapes. Pinot Blanc is the most affordable – and is well worth looking out for. The 'noble' grape varieties of the region are Gewürztraminer, Muscat, Riesling and Pinot Gris and they are always made on a single-variety basis. The richest, most exotic wines are those from individual *grand cru* vineyards, which are named on the label. Some *vendange tardive* (late harvest) wines are made, but tend to be expensive. All the wines are sold in tall, slim green bottles known as flûtes that closely resemble those of the Mosel, and the names of producers and grape varieties are often German too, so it is widely assumed that Alsace wines are German in style, if not in nationality. But this is not the case in either particular. Alsace wines are dry and quite unique in character – and definitely French.

Amarone – Style of red wine made in Valpolicella, Italy. Specially selected grapes are held back from the harvest and stored for several months to dry them out. They are then pressed and fermented into a highly concentrated speciality dry wine. Amarone means 'bitter', describing the dry style of the flavour.

amontillado – *See* sherry.

aperitif – If a wine is thus described, I believe it will give more pleasure before a meal than with one. Crisp, low-alcohol German wines and other delicately flavoured whites (including many dry Italians) are examples.

Appellation d'Origine Contrôlée – Commonly abbreviated to AC or AOC, this is the system under which quality wines are defined in France. About a third of the country's vast annual output qualifies, and there are more than 400 distinct AC zones. The declaration of an AC on the label signifies that the wine meets standards concerning location of vineyards and wineries, grape varieties and limits on harvest per hectare, methods of cultivation and vinification, and alcohol content. Wines are inspected and tasted by state-appointed committees. The one major aspect of any given wine that an AC cannot guarantee is that you will like it – but it certainly improves the chances.

Appellation d'Origine Protégée (AOP) – Under recent EU rule changes, the AOC system is gradually transforming into AOP. In effect, it will mean little more than the exchange of 'controlled' with 'protected' on labels. One quirk of the new rules is that makers of AOP wines will be able to name the constituent grape variety or varieties on their labels, if they so wish.

Apulia – Anglicised name for Puglia.

Aragones – Synonym in Portugal, especially in the Alentejo region, for the Tempranillo grape variety of Spain.

Ardèche – Region of southern France to the west of the Rhône valley, home to a good vin de pays zone known as the Coteaux de L'Ardèche. Lots of decent-value reds from Syrah grapes, and some, less interesting, dry whites.

Arneis – White grape variety of Piedmont, north-west Italy. Makes dry whites with a certain almondy richness at often-inflated prices.

Assyrtiko – White grape variety of Greece now commonly named on dry white wines, sometimes of great quality, from the mainland and islands.

Asti – Town and major winemaking centre in Piedmont, Italy. The sparkling (spumante) sweet wines made from Moscato grapes are inexpensive and often delicious. Typical alcohol level is a modest 5 to 7 per cent.

attack – In wine tasting, the first impression made by the wine in the mouth.

Auslese – German wine-quality designation. *See* QmP.

B

Baga – Black grape variety indigenous to Portugal. Makes famously concentrated, juicy reds that get their deep colour from the grape's particularly thick skins. Look out for this name, now quite frequently quoted as the varietal on Portuguese wine labels. Often very good value for money.

balance – A big word in the vocabulary of wine tasting. Respectable wine must get two key things right: lots of fruitiness from the sweet grape juice, and plenty of acidity so the sweetness is 'balanced' with the crispness familiar in good dry whites and the dryness that marks out good reds. Some wines are noticeably 'well balanced' in that they have memorable fruitiness and the clean, satisfying 'finish' (last flavour in the mouth) that ideal acidity imparts.

Barbera – Black grape variety originally of Piedmont in Italy. Most commonly seen as Barbera d'Asti, the vigorously fruity red wine made around Asti – once better known for sweet sparkling Asti Spumante. Barbera grapes are now being grown in South America, often producing a sleeker, smoother style than at home in Italy.

Bardolino – Once fashionable, light red wine DOC of Veneto, north-west Italy. Bardolino is made principally from Corvina Veronese grapes plus Rondinella, Molinara and Negrara. Best wines are supposed to be those labelled Bardolino Superiore, a DOCG created in 2002. This classification closely specifies the permissible grape varieties and sets the alcohol level at a minimum of 12 per cent.

Barossa Valley – Famed vineyard region north of Adelaide, Australia, produces hearty reds principally from Shiraz, Cabernet Sauvignon and Grenache grapes, plus plenty of lush white wine from Chardonnay. Also known for limey, long-lived, mineral dry whites from Riesling grapes.

barrique – Barrel in French. *En barrique* on a wine label signifies the wine has been matured in oak.

Beaujolais – Unique red wines from the southern reaches of Burgundy, France, are made from Gamay grapes. Beaujolais nouveau, now deeply unfashionable, provides a friendly introduction to the bouncy, red-fruit style of the wine, but for the authentic experience, go for Beaujolais Villages, from the region's better, northern vineyards. There are ten AC zones within this northern sector making wines under their own names. Known as the *crus*, these are Brouilly, Chénas, Chiroubles, Côte de Brouilly, Fleurie, Juliénas, Morgon, Moulin à Vent, Regnié and St Amour and produce most of the best wines of the region. Prices are higher than those for Beaujolais Villages, but by no means always justifiably so.

Beaumes de Venise – Village near Châteauneuf du Pape in France's Rhône valley, famous for sweet and alcoholic wine from Muscat grapes. Delicious, grapey wines. A small number of growers also make strong (sometimes rather tough) red wines under the village name.

Beaune – One of the two winemaking centres (the other is Nuits St Georges) at the heart of Burgundy in France. Three of the region's humbler appellations take the name of the town: Côtes de Beaune, Côtes de Beaune Villages and Hautes Côtes de Beaune. Wines made under these ACs are often, but by no means always, good value for money.

berry fruit – Some red wines deliver a burst of flavour in the mouth that corresponds to biting into a newly picked berry – strawberry, blackberry, etc. So a wine described as having berry fruit (by this writer, anyway) has freshness, liveliness and immediate appeal.

bianco – White wine, Italy.

Bical – White grape variety principally of Dão region of northern Portugal. Not usually identified on labels, because most of it goes into inexpensive sparkling wines. Can make still wines of very refreshing crispness.

biodynamics – A cultivation method taking the organic approach several steps further. Biodynamic winemakers plant and tend their vineyards according to a date and time calendar 'in harmony' with the movements of the planets. Some of France's best-known wine estates subscribe, and many more are going that way. It might all sound bonkers, but it's salutary to learn that biodynamics is based on principles first described by a very eminent man, the Austrian educationist Rudolph Steiner. He's lately been in the news for having written, in 1919, that farmers crazy enough to feed animal products to cattle would drive the livestock 'mad'.

bite – In wine tasting, the impression on the palate of a wine with plenty of acidity and, often, tannin.

blanc – White wine, France.

blanc de blancs – White wine from white grapes, France. May seem to be stating the obvious, but some white wines (e.g. champagne) are made, partially or entirely, from black grapes.

blanc de noirs – White wine from black grapes, France. Usually sparkling (especially champagne) made from black Pinot Meunier and Pinot Noir grapes, with no Chardonnay or other white varieties.

blanco – White wine, Spain and Portugal.

Blauer Zweigelt – Black grape variety of Austria, making a large proportion of the country's red wines, some of excellent quality.

Bobal – Black grape variety mostly of south-eastern Spain. Thick skin is good for colour and juice contributes acidity to blends.

bodega – In Spain, a wine producer or wine shop.

Bonarda – Black grape variety of northern Italy. Now more widely planted in Argentina, where it makes rather elegant red wines, often representing great value.

botrytis – Full name, *botrytis cinerea*, is that of a beneficent fungus that can attack ripe grape bunches late in the season, shrivelling the berries to a gruesome-looking mess, which yields concentrated juice of prized sweetness. Cheerfully known as 'noble rot', this fungus is actively encouraged by winemakers in regions as diverse as Sauternes (in Bordeaux), Monbazillac (in Bergerac), the Rhine and Mosel valleys, Hungary's Tokaji region and South Australia to make ambrosial dessert wines.

bouncy – The feel in the mouth of a red wine with young, juicy fruitiness. Good Beaujolais is bouncy, as are many north-west-Italian wines from Barbera and Dolcetto grapes.

Bourgogne Grand Ordinaire – Former AC of Burgundy, France. *See* Coteaux Bourguignons.

Bourgueil – Appellation of Loire Valley, France. Long-lived red wines from Cabernet Franc grapes.

briary – In wine tasting, associated with the flavours of fruit from prickly bushes such as blackberries.

brûlé – Pleasant burnt-toffee taste or smell, as in crème brûlée.

brut – Driest style of sparkling wine. Originally French, for very dry champagnes specially developed for the British market, but now used for sparkling wines from all round the world.

Buzet – Little-seen AC of south-west France overshadowed by Bordeaux but producing some characterful ripe reds.

C

Cabardès – AC for red and rosé wines from area north of Carcassonne, Aude, France. Principally Cabernet Sauvignon and Merlot grapes.

Cabernet Franc – Black grape variety originally of France. It makes the light-bodied and keenly edged red wines of the Loire Valley – such as Chinon and Saumur. And it is much grown in Bordeaux, especially in the appellation of St Emilion. Also now planted in Argentina, Australia and North America. Wines, especially in the Loire, are characterised by a leafy, sappy style and bold fruitiness. Most are best enjoyed young.

Cabernet Sauvignon – Black (or, rather, blue) grape variety now grown in virtually every wine-producing nation. When perfectly ripened, the grapes are smaller than many other varieties and have particularly thick skins. This means that when pressed, Cabernet grapes have a high proportion of skin to juice – and that makes for wine with lots of colour and tannin. In Bordeaux, the grape's traditional home, the grandest Cabernet-based wines have always been known as *vins de garde* (wines to keep) because they take years, even decades, to evolve as the effect of all that skin extraction preserves the fruit all the way to magnificent maturity. But in today's impatient world, these grapes are exploited in modern winemaking techniques to produce the sublime flavours of mature Cabernet without having to hang around for lengthy periods awaiting maturation. While there's nothing like a fine, ten-year-old claret (and nothing quite as expensive), there are many excellent Cabernets from around the world that amply illustrate this grape's characteristics. Classic smells and flavours include blackcurrants, cedar wood, chocolate, tobacco – even violets.

Cahors – An AC of the Lot Valley in south-west France once famous for 'black wine'. This was a curious concoction of straightforward wine mixed with a soupy must, made by boiling up new-pressed juice to concentrate it (through evaporation) before fermentation. The myth is still perpetuated that Cahors wine continues to be made in this way, but production on this basis actually ceased 150 years ago. Cahors today is no stronger, or blacker, than the wines of neighbouring appellations.

Cairanne – Village of the appellation collectively known as the Côtes du Rhône in southern France. Cairanne is one of several villages entitled to put their name on the labels of wines made within their AC boundary, and the appearance of this name is quite reliably an indicator of a very good wine indeed.

Calatayud – DO (quality wine zone) near Zaragoza in the Aragon region of northern Spain where they're making some astonishingly good wines at bargain prices, mainly reds from Garnacha and Tempranillo grapes. These are the varieties that go into the light and oaky wines of Rioja, but in Calatayud, the wines are dark, dense and decidedly different.

Cannonau – Black grape native to Sardinia by name, but in fact the same variety as the ubiquitous Grenache of France (and Garnacha of Spain).

cantina sociale – *See* co-op.

Carignan – Black grape variety of Mediterranean France. It is rarely identified on labels, but is a major constituent of wines from the southern Rhône and Languedoc-Roussillon regions. Known as Carignano in Italy and Cariñena in Spain.

Cariñena – A region of north-east Spain, south of Navarra, known for substantial reds, as well as the Spanish name for the Carignan grape (*qv*).

Carmenère – Black grape variety once widely grown in Bordeaux but abandoned due to cultivation problems. Lately revived in South America where it is producing fine wines, sometimes with echoes of Bordeaux.

cassis – As a tasting note, signifies a wine that has a noticeable blackcurrant-concentrate flavour or smell. Much associated with the Cabernet Sauvignon grape.

Castelao – Portuguese black grape variety. Same as Periquita.

Catarratto – White grape variety of Sicily. In skilled hands it can make anything from keen, green-fruit dry whites to lush, oaked super-ripe styles. Also used for Marsala.

cat's pee – In tasting notes, a mildly jocular reference to a certain style of Sauvignon Blanc wine.

cava – The sparkling wine of Spain. Most originates in Catalonia, but the Denominación de Origen (DO) guarantee of authenticity is open to producers in many regions of the country. Much cava is very reasonably priced even though it is made by the same method as champagne – second fermentation in bottle, known in Spain as the *método clásico*.

CdR – Côtes du Rhône.

Cépage – Grape variety, French. 'Cépage Merlot' on a label simply means the wine is made largely or exclusively from Merlot grapes.

Chablis – Northernmost AC of France's Burgundy region. Its dry white wines from Chardonnay grapes are known for their fresh and steely style, but the best wines also age very gracefully into complex classics.

Chambourcin – Sounds like a cream cheese but it's a relatively modern (1963) French hybrid black grape that makes some good non-appellation lightweight-but-concentrated reds in the Loire Valley and now some heftier versions in Australia.

Chardonnay – The world's most popular grape variety. Said to originate from the village of Chardonnay in the Mâconnais region of southern Burgundy, the vine is now planted in every wine-producing nation. Wines are commonly characterised by generous colour and sweet-apple smell, but styles range from lean and sharp to opulently rich. Australia started the craze for oaked Chardonnay, the gold-coloured, super-ripe, buttery 'upfront' wines that are a caricature of lavish and outrageously expensive burgundies such as Meursault and Puligny-Montrachet. Rich to the point of egginess, these Aussie pretenders are now giving way to a sleeker, more minerally style with much less oak presence – if any at all. California and Chile, New Zealand and South Africa are competing hard to imitate the Burgundian style, and Australia's success in doing so.

Châteauneuf du Pape – Famed appellation centred on a picturesque village of the southern Rhône valley in France where in the 1320s French Pope Clement V had a splendid new château built for himself as a country retreat amidst his vineyards. The red wines of the AC, which can be made from 13 different grape varieties but principally Grenache, Syrah and Mourvèdre, are regarded as the best of the southern Rhône and have become rather expensive – but they can be sensationally good. Expensive white wines are also made.

Chenin Blanc – White grape variety of the Loire Valley, France. Now also grown farther afield, especially in South Africa. Makes dry, soft white wines and also rich, sweet styles. Sadly, many low-cost Chenin wines are bland and uninteresting.

cherry – In wine tasting, either a pale red colour or, more commonly, a smell or flavour akin to the sun-warmed, bursting sweet ripeness of cherries. Many Italian wines, from lightweights such as Bardolino and Valpolicella to serious Chianti, have this character. 'Black cherry' as a description is often used of Merlot wines – meaning they are sweet but have a firmness associated with the thicker skins of black cherries.

Cinsault – Black grape variety of southern France, where it is invariably blended with others in wines of all qualities ranging from vin de pays to the pricy reds of Châteauneuf du Pape. Also much planted in South Africa. The effect in wine is to add keen aromas (sometimes compared with turpentine!) and softness to the blend. The name is often spelt Cinsaut.

Clape, La – A small *cru* (defined quality-vineyard area) within the Coteaux du Languedoc where the growers make some seriously delicious red wines, mainly from Carignan, Grenache and Syrah grapes. A name worth looking out for on labels from the region.

claret – The red wine of Bordeaux, France. It comes from Latin *clarus*, meaning 'clear', recalling a time when the red wines of the region were much lighter in colour than they are now.

clarete – On Spanish labels indicates a pale-coloured red wine. Tinto signifies a deeper hue.

classed growth – English translation of French *cru classé* describes a group of 60 individual wine estates in the Médoc district of Bordeaux, which in 1855 were granted this new status on the basis that their wines were the most expensive at that time. The classification was a promotional wheeze to attract attention to the Bordeaux stand at that year's Great Exhibition in Paris. Amazingly, all of the 60 wines concerned are still in production and most still occupy more or less their original places in the pecking order price-wise. The league was divided up into five divisions from *Premier Grand Cru Classé* (just four wines originally, with one promoted in 1971 – the only change ever made to the classification) to *Cinquième Grand Cru Classé*. Other regions of Bordeaux, notably Graves and St Emilion, have since imitated Médoc and introduced their own rankings of *cru classé* estates.

classic – An overused term in every respect – wine descriptions being no exception. In this book, the word is used to describe a very good wine of its type. So, a 'classic' Cabernet Sauvignon is one that is recognisably and admirably characteristic of that grape.

Classico – Under Italy's wine laws, this word appended to the name of a DOC zone has an important significance. The classico wines of the region can only be made from vineyards lying in the best-rated areas, and wines thus labelled (e.g. Chianti Classico, Soave Classico, Valpolicella Classico) can be reliably counted on to be a cut above the rest.

Colombard – White grape variety of southern France. Once employed almost entirely for making the wine that is distilled for armagnac and cognac brandies, but lately restored to varietal prominence in the Vin de Pays des Côtes de Gascogne where high-tech wineries turn it into a fresh and crisp, if unchallenging, dry wine at a budget price. But beware, cheap Colombard (especially from South Africa) can still be very dull.

Conca de Barbera – Winemaking region of Catalonia, Spain.

co-op – Very many of France's good-quality, inexpensive wines are made by co-operatives. These are wine-producing factories whose members, and joint-owners, are local *vignerons* (vine growers). Each year they sell their harvests to the co-op for turning into branded wines. In Italy, co-op wines can be identified by the words *Cantina Sociale* on the label and in Germany by the term *Winzergenossenschaft*.

Corbières – A name to look out for. It's an AC of France's Midi (deep south) and produces countless robust reds and a few interesting whites, often at bargain prices.

Cortese – White grape variety of Piedmont, Italy. At its best, makes amazingly delicious, keenly brisk and fascinating wines, including those of the Gavi DOCG. Worth seeking out.

Costières de Nîmes – Until 1989, this AC of southern France was known as the Costières de Gard. It forms a buffer between the southern Rhône and Languedoc-Roussillon regions, and makes wines from broadly the same range of grape varieties. It's a name to look out for, the best red wines being notable for their concentration of colour and fruit, with the earthy-spiciness of the better Rhône wines and a likeable liquorice note. A few good white wines, too, and even a decent rosé or two.

Côte – In French, it simply means a side, or slope, of a hill. The implication in wine terms is that the grapes come from a vineyard ideally situated for maximum sunlight, good drainage and the unique soil conditions prevailing on the hill in question. It's fair enough to claim that vines grown on slopes might get more sunlight than those grown on the flat, but there is no guarantee whatsoever that any wine labelled 'Côtes du' this or that is made from grapes grown on a hillside anyway. Côtes du Rhône wines are a case in point. Many 'Côtes' wines come from entirely level vineyards and it is worth remembering that many of the vineyards of Bordeaux, producing most of the world's priciest wines, are little short of prairie-flat. The quality factor is determined much more significantly by the weather and the talents of the winemaker.

Coteaux Bourguignons – Generic AC of Burgundy, France, since 2011 for red and rosé wines from Pinot Noir and Gamay grapes, and white wines from (principally) Chardonnay and Bourgogne Aligoté grapes. The AC replaces the former appellation Bourgogne Grand Ordinaire.

Côtes de Blaye – Appellation Contrôlée zone of Bordeaux on the right bank of the River Gironde, opposite the more prestigious Médoc zone of the left bank. Best-rated vineyards qualify for the AC Premières Côtes de Blaye. A couple of centuries ago, Blaye (pronounced 'bligh') was the grander of the two, and even today makes some wines that compete well for quality, and at a fraction of the price of wines from its more fashionable rival across the water.

Côtes de Bourg – AC neighbouring Côtes de Blaye, making red wines of fast-improving quality and value.

Côtes du Luberon – Appellation Contrôlée zone of Provence in south-east France. Wines, mostly red, are similar in style to Côtes du Rhône.

Côtes du Rhône – One of the biggest and best-known appellations of south-east France, covering an area roughly defined by the southern reaches of the valley of the River Rhône. Long notorious for cheap and execrable reds, the Côtes du Rhône AC has lately achieved remarkable improvements in quality at all points along the price scale. Lots of brilliant-value warm and spicy reds, principally from Grenache and Syrah grapes. There are also some white and rosé wines.

Côtes du Rhône Villages – Appellation within the larger Côtes du Rhône AC for wine of supposed superiority made in a number of zones associated with a long list of nominated individual villages.

Côtes du Roussillon – Huge appellation of south-west France known for strong, dark, peppery reds often offering very decent value.

Côtes du Roussillon Villages – Appellation for superior wines from a number of nominated locations within the larger Roussillon AC. Some of these village wines can be of exceptional quality and value.

crianza – Means 'nursery' in Spanish. On Rioja and Navarra wines, the designation signifies a wine that has been nursed through a maturing period of at least a year in oak casks and a further six months in bottle before being released for sale.

cru – A word that crops up with confusing regularity on French wine labels. It means 'the growing' or 'the making' of a wine and asserts that the wine concerned is from a specific vineyard. Under the Appellation Contrôlée rules, countless *crus* are classified in various hierarchical ranks. Hundreds of individual vineyards are described as *premier cru* or *grand cru* in the classic wine regions of Alsace, Bordeaux, Burgundy and Champagne. The common denominator is that the wine can be counted on to be enormously expensive. On humbler wines, the use of the word *cru* tends to be mere decoration.

cru classé – *See* classed growth.

cuve – A vat for wine. French.

cuvée – French for the wine in a *cuve*, or vat. The word is much used on labels to imply that the wine is from just one vat, and thus of unique, unblended character. *Première cuvée* is supposedly the best wine from a given pressing because the grapes have had only the initial, gentle squashing to extract the free-run juice. Subsequent *cuvées* will have been from harsher pressings, grinding the grape pulp to extract the last drop of juice.

D

Dão – Major wine-producing region of northern Portugal now turning out much more interesting reds than it used to – worth looking out for anything made by mega-producer Sogrape.

demi sec – 'Half-dry' style of French (and some other) wines. Beware. It can mean anything from off-dry to cloyingly sweet.

DO – Denominación de Origen, Spain's wine-regulating scheme, similar to France's AC, but older – the first DO region was Rioja, from 1926. DO wines are Spain's best, accounting for a third of the nation's annual production.

DOC – Stands for Denominazione di Origine Controllata, Italy's equivalent of France's AC. The wines are made according to the stipulations of each of the system's 300-plus denominated zones of origin, along with a further 73 zones, which enjoy the superior classification of DOCG (DOC with *e Garantita* – guaranteed – appended).

Durif – Rare black grape variety mostly of California, where it is also known as Petite Sirah, but with some plantings in Australia.

E

earthy – A tricky word in the wine vocabulary. In this book, its use is meant to be complimentary. It indicates that the wine somehow suggests the soil the grapes were grown in, even (perhaps a shade too poetically) the landscape in which the vineyards lie. The amazing-value red wines of the torrid, volcanic southernmost regions of Italy are often described as earthy. This is an association with the pleasantly 'scorched' back-flavour in wines made from the ultra-ripe harvests of this near-sub-tropical part of the world.

edge – A wine with edge is one with evident (although not excessive) acidity.

élevé – 'Brought up' in French. Much used on wine labels where the wine has been matured (brought up) in oak barrels, *élevé en fûts de chêne*, to give it extra dimensions.

Entre Deux Mers – Meaning 'between two seas', it's a region lying between the Dordogne and Garonne rivers of Bordeaux, now mainly known for dry white wines from Sauvignon and Semillon grapes.

Estremadura – Wine-producing region occupying Portugal's coastal area north of Lisbon. Lots of interesting wines from indigenous grape varieties, usually at bargain prices. If a label mentions Estremadura, it is a safe rule that there might be something good within.

Extremadura – Minor wine-producing region of western Spain abutting the frontier with Portugal's Alentejo region. Not to be confused with Estremadura of Portugal (above).

F

Falanghina – Revived ancient grape variety of southern Italy now making some superbly fresh and tangy white wines.

Faugères – AC of the Languedoc in south-west France. Source of many hearty, economic reds.

Feteasca – White grape variety widely grown in Romania. Name means 'maiden's grape' and the wine tends to be soft and slightly sweet.

Fiano – White grape variety of the Campania of southern Italy and Sicily, lately revived. It is said to have been cultivated by the ancient Romans for a wine called Apianum.

finish – The last flavour lingering in the mouth after wine has been swallowed.

fino – Pale and very dry style of sherry. You drink it thoroughly chilled – and you don't keep it any longer after opening than other dry white wines. Needs to be fresh to be at its best.

Fitou – One of the first 'designer' wines, it's an appellation in France's Languedoc region, where production is dominated by one huge co-operative, the Vignerons de Mont Tauch. Back in the 1970s, this co-op paid a corporate-image company to come up with a Fitou logo and label-design style, and the wines have prospered ever since. And it's not just packaging – Fitou at all price levels can be very good value, especially from the Mont Tauch co-op.

flabby – Fun word describing a wine that tastes dilute or watery, with insufficient acidity.

Frappato – Black grape variety of Sicily. Light red wines.

fruit – In tasting terms, the fruit is the greater part of the overall flavour of a wine. The wine is (or should be) after all, composed entirely of fruit.

G

Gamay – The black grape that makes all red Beaujolais and some ordinary burgundy. It is a pretty safe rule to avoid Gamay wines from any other region, but there are exceptions.

Garganega – White grape variety of the Veneto region of north-east Italy. Best known as the principal ingredient of Soave, but occasionally included in varietal blends and mentioned as such on labels. Correctly pronounced 'gar-GAN-iga'.

Garnacha – Spanish black grape variety synonymous with Grenache of France. It is blended with Tempranillo to make the red wines of Rioja and Navarra, and is now quite widely cultivated elsewhere in Spain to make grippingly fruity varietals.

garrigue – Arid land of France's deep south giving its name to a style of red wine that notionally evokes the herby, heated, peppery flavours associated with such a landscape. A tricky metaphor!

Gavi – DOCG for dry but rich white wine from Cortese grapes in Piedmont, north-west Italy. Trendy Gavi di Gavi wines tend to be enjoyably lush, but are rather expensive.

Gewürztraminer – One of the great grape varieties of Alsace, France. At their best, the wines are perfumed with lychees and are richly, spicily fruity, yet quite dry. Gewürztraminer from Alsace can be expensive, but the grape is also grown with some success in Germany, Italy, New Zealand and South America, at more approachable prices. Pronounced 'ge-VOORTS-traminner'.

Givry – AC for red and white wines in the Côte Chalonnaise sub-region of Burgundy. Source of some wonderfully natural-tasting reds that might be lighter than those of the more prestigious Côte d'Or to the north, but have great merits of their own. Relatively, the wines are often underpriced.

Glera – Alternative name for Prosecco grape of northern Italy.

Godello – White grape variety of Galicia, Spain.

Graciano – Black grape variety of Spain that is one of the minor constituents of Rioja. Better known in its own right in Australia where it can make dense, spicy, long-lived red wines.

green – I don't often use this in the pejorative. Green, to me, is a likeable degree of freshness, especially in Sauvignon Blanc wines.

Grecanico – White grape variety of southern Italy, especially Sicily. Aromatic, grassy dry white wines.

Greco – White grape variety of southern Italy believed to be of ancient Greek origin. Big-flavoured dry white wines.

Grenache – The mainstay of the wines of the southern Rhône Valley in France. Grenache is usually the greater part of the mix in Côtes du Rhône reds and is widely planted right across the neighbouring Languedoc-Roussillon region. It's a big-cropping variety that thrives even in the hottest climates and is really a blending grape – most commonly with Syrah, the noble variety of the northern Rhône. Few French wines are labelled with its name, but the grape has caught on in Australia in a big way and it is now becoming a familiar varietal, known for strong, dark liquorous reds. Grenache is the French name for what is originally a Spanish variety, Garnacha.

Grillo – White grape of Sicily said to be among the island's oldest indigenous varieties, pre-dating the arrival of the Greeks in 600 BC. Much used for fortified Marsala, it has lately been revived for interesting, aromatic dry table wines.

grip – In wine-tasting terminology, the sensation in the mouth produced by a wine that has a healthy quantity of tannin in it. A wine with grip is a good wine. A wine with too much tannin, or which is still too young (the tannin hasn't 'softened' with age) is not described as having grip, but as mouth-puckering – or simply undrinkable.

Grolleau – Black grape variety of the Loire Valley principally cultivated for Rosé d'Anjou.

Gros Plant – White grape variety of the Pays Nantais in France's Loire estuary; synonymous with the Folle Blanche grape of south-west France.

Grüner Veltliner – The 'national' white-wine grape of Austria. In the past it made mostly soft, German-style everyday wines, but now is behind some excellent dry styles, too.

H

halbtrocken – 'Half-dry' in Germany's wine vocabulary. A reassurance that the wine is not some ghastly sugared Liebfraumilch-style confection.

hard – In red wine, a flavour denoting excess tannin, probably due to immaturity.

Haut-Médoc – Extensive AOC of Bordeaux accounting for the greater part of the vineyard area to the north of the city of Bordeaux and west of the Gironde river. The Haut-Médoc incorporates the prestigious commune-AOCs of Listrac, Margaux, Moulis, Pauillac, St Estephe and St Julien.

hock – The wine of Germany's Rhine river valleys. Traditionally, but no longer consistently, it comes in brown bottles, as distinct from the wine of the Mosel river valleys – which comes in green ones.

I

Indication Géographique Protégée (IGP) – Introduced to France in 2010 under new EU-wide wine-designation rules, IGP covers the wines hitherto known as vins de pays. Some wines are already being labelled IGP, but established vins de pays producers are unlikely to redesignate their products in a hurry, and are not obliged to do so. Some will abbreviate, so, for example, Vin de Pays d'Oc shortens to Pays d'Oc.

Indicazione Geografica Tipica – Italian wine-quality designation, broadly equivalent to France's vin de pays. The label has to state the geographical location of the vineyard and will often (but not always) state the principal grape varieties from which the wine is made.

isinglass – A gelatinous material used in fining (clarifying) wine. It is derived from fish bladders and consequently is eschewed by makers of 'vegetarian' wines.

J

jammy – The 'sweetness' in dry red wines is supposed to evoke ripeness rather than sugariness. Sometimes, flavours include a sweetness reminiscent of jam. Usually a fault in the winemaking technique.

Jerez – Wine town of Andalucia, Spain, and home to sherry. The English word 'sherry' is a simple mispronunciation of Jerez.

joven – Young wine, Spanish. In regions such as Rioja, *vino joven* is a synonym for *sin crianza*, which means 'without ageing' in cask or bottle.

Jura – Wine region of eastern France incorporating four AOCs, Arbois, Château-Chalon, Côtes du Jura and L'Etoile. Known for still red, white and rosé wines and sparkling wines as well as exotic *vin de paille* and *vin jaune*.

Jurançon – Appellation for white wines from Courbu and Manseng grapes at Pau, south-west France.

K

Kabinett – Under Germany's bewildering wine-quality rules, this is a classification of a top-quality (QmP) wine. Expect a keen, dry, racy style. The name comes from the cabinet or cupboard in which winemakers traditionally kept their most treasured bottles.

Kekfrankos – Black grape variety of Hungary, particularly the Sopron region, which makes some of the country's more interesting red wines, characterised by colour and spiciness. Same variety as Austria's Blaufrankisch.

L

Ladoix – Unfashionable AC at northern edge of Côtes de Beaune makes some of Burgundy's true bargain reds. A name to look out for.

Lambrusco – The name is that of a black grape variety widely grown across northern Italy. True Lambrusco wine is red, dry and very slightly sparkling, but from the 1980s Britain was deluged with a strange, sweet manifestation of the style, which has done little to enhance the good name of the original. Good Lambrusco is delicious and fun, but in this country now very hard to find.

Languedoc-Roussillon – Vast area of southern France, including the country's south-west Mediterranean region. The source, now, of many great-value wines from countless ACs and vin de pays zones.

lees – The detritus of the winemaking process that collects in the bottom of the vat or cask. Wines left for extended periods on the lees can acquire extra dimensions of flavour, in particular a 'leesy' creaminess.

legs – The liquid residue left clinging to the sides of the glass after wine has been swirled. The persistence of the legs is an indicator of the weight of alcohol. Also known as 'tears'.

lieu dit – This is starting to appear on French wine labels. It translates as an 'agreed place' and is an area of vineyard defined as of particular character or merit, but not classified under wine law. Usually, the *lieu dit*'s name is stated, with the implication that the wine in question has special value.

liquorice – The pungent, slightly burnt flavours of this once-fashionable confection are detectable in some wines made from very ripe grapes, for example, the Malbec harvested in Argentina and several varieties grown in the very hot vineyards of southernmost Italy. A close synonym is 'tarry'. This characteristic is by no means a fault in red wine, unless very dominant, but it can make for a challenging flavour that might not appeal to all tastes.

liquorous – Wines of great weight and glyceriney texture (evidenced by the 'legs', or 'tears', which cling to the glass after the wine has been swirled) are always noteworthy. The connection with liquor is drawn in respect of the feel of the wine in the mouth, rather than with the higher alcoholic strength of spirits.

Lirac – Village and AOC of southern Rhône Valley, France. A near-neighbour of the esteemed appellation of Châteauneuf du Pape, Lirac makes red wine of comparable depth and complexity, at competitive prices.

Lugana – DOC of Lombardy, Italy, known for a dry white wine that is often of real distinction – rich, almondy stuff from the ubiquitous Trebbiano grape.

M

Macabeo – One of the main grapes used for cava, the sparkling wine of Spain. It is the same grape as Viura.

Mâcon – Town and collective appellation of southern Burgundy, France. Lightweight white wines from Chardonnay grapes and similarly light reds from Pinot Noir and some Gamay. The better ones, and the ones exported, have the AC Mâcon-Villages and there are individual village wines with their own ACs including Mâcon-Clessé, Mâcon-Viré and Mâcon-Lugny.

Malbec – Black grape variety grown on a small scale in Bordeaux, and the mainstay of the wines of Cahors in France's Dordogne region under the name Cot. Now much better known for producing big butch reds in Argentina.

manzanilla – Pale, very dry sherry of Sanlucar de Barrameda, a resort town on the Bay of Cadiz in Spain. Manzanilla is proud to be distinct from the pale, very dry fino sherry of the main producing town of Jerez de la Frontera an hour's drive inland. Drink it chilled and fresh – it goes downhill in an opened bottle after just a few days, even if kept (as it should be) in the fridge.

Margaret River – Vineyard region of Western Australia regarded as ideal for grape varieties including Cabernet Sauvignon. It has a relatively cool climate and a reputation for making sophisticated wines, both red and white.

Marlborough – Best-known vineyard region of New Zealand's South Island has a cool climate and a name for brisk but cerebral Sauvignon Blanc and Chardonnay wines.

Marsanne – White grape variety of the northern Rhône Valley and, increasingly, of the wider south of France. It's known for making well-coloured wines with heady aroma and fruit.

Mataro – Black grape variety of Australia. It's the same as the Mourvèdre of France and Monastrell of Spain.

Mazuelo – Spanish name for France's black grape variety Carignan.

McLaren Vale – Vineyard region south of Adelaide in south-east Australia. Known for blockbuster Shiraz (and Chardonnay) that can be of great balance and quality from winemakers who keep the ripeness under control.

meaty – Weighty, rich red wine style.

Mencia – Black grape variety of Galicia and north-west Spain. Light red wines.

Mendoza – The region to watch in Argentina. Lying to the east of the Andes mountains, just about opposite the best vineyards of Chile on the other side, Mendoza accounts for the bulk of Argentine wine production, with quality improving fast.

Merlot – One of the great black wine grapes of Bordeaux, and now grown all over the world. The name is said to derive from the French *merle*, meaning a blackbird. Characteristics of Merlot-based wines attract descriptions such as 'plummy' and 'plump' with black-cherry aroma. The grapes are larger than most, and thus have less skin in proportion to their flesh. This means the resulting wines have less tannin than wines from smaller-berry varieties such as Cabernet Sauvignon, and are therefore, in the Bordeaux context at least, more suitable for drinking while still relatively young.

middle palate – In wine tasting, the impression given by the wine when it is held in the mouth.

Midi – Catch-all term for the deep south of France west of the Rhône Valley.

mineral – I am trying to excise this overused word from my notes, but not so far managing to do so with much conviction. To me it evokes flavours such as the stone-pure freshness of some Loire dry whites, or the steely quality of the more austere style of the Chardonnay grape, especially in Chablis. Mineral really just means something mined, as in dug out of the ground, like iron ore (as in steel) or rock, as in, er, stone. Maybe there's something in it, but I am not entirely confident.

Minervois – AC for (mostly) red wines from vineyards around the town of Minerve in the Languedoc-Roussillon region of France. Often good value. The new Minervois La Livinière AC – a sort of Minervois *grand cru* – is host to some great estates including Château Maris and Vignobles Lorgeril.

Monastrell – Black grape variety of Spain, widely planted in Mediterranean regions for inexpensive wines notable for their high alcohol and toughness – though they can mature into excellent, soft reds. The variety is known in France as Mourvèdre and in Australia as Mataro.

Monbazillac – AC for sweet, dessert wines within the wider appellation of Bergerac in south-west France. Made from the same grape varieties (principally Sauvignon and Semillon) that go into the much costlier counterpart wines of Barsac and Sauternes near Bordeaux, these stickies from botrytis-affected, late-harvested grapes can be delicious and good value for money.

Montalcino – Hill town of Tuscany, Italy, and a DOCG for strong and very long-lived red wines from Brunello grapes. The wines are mostly very expensive. Rosso di Montalcino, a DOC for the humbler wines of the zone, is often a good buy.

Montepulciano – Black grape variety of Italy. Best known in Montepulciano d'Abruzzo, the juicy, purply-black and bramble-fruited red of the Abruzzi region midway down Italy's Adriatic side. Also the grape in the rightly popular hearty reds of Rosso Conero from around Ancona in the Marches. Not to be confused with the hill town of Montepulciano in Tuscany, famous for expensive Vino Nobile di Montepulciano wine.

morello – Lots of red wines have smells and flavours redolent of cherries. Morello cherries, among the darkest coloured and sweetest of all varieties and the preferred choice of cherry-brandy producers, have a distinct sweetness resembled by some wines made from Merlot grapes. A morello whiff or taste is generally very welcome.

Moscatel – Spanish Muscat.

Moscato – *See* Muscat.

Moselle – The wine of Germany's Mosel river valleys, collectively known for winemaking purposes as Mosel-Saar-Ruwer. The wine always comes in slim, green bottles, as distinct from the brown bottles traditionally, but no longer exclusively, employed for Rhine wines.

Mourvèdre – Widely planted black grape variety of southern France. It's an ingredient in many of the wines of Provence, the Rhône and Languedoc, including the ubiquitous Vin de Pays d'Oc. It's a hot-climate vine and the wine is usually blended with other varieties to give sweet aromas and 'backbone' to the mix. Known as Mataro in Australia and Monastrell in Spain.

Muscadet – One of France's most familiar everyday whites, made from a grape called the Melon or Melon de Bourgogne. It comes from vineyards at the estuarial end of the River Loire, and has a sea-breezy freshness about it. The better wines are reckoned to be those from the vineyards in the Sèvre et Maine region, and many are made *sur lie* – 'on the lees' – meaning that the wine is left in contact with the yeasty deposit of its fermentation until just before bottling, in an endeavour to add interest to what can sometimes be an acidic and fruitless style.

Muscat – Grape variety with origins in ancient Greece, and still grown widely among the Aegean islands for the production of sweet white wines. Muscats are the wines that taste more like grape juice than any other – but the high sugar levels ensure they are also among the most alcoholic of wines, too. Known as Moscato in Italy, the grape is much used for making sweet sparkling wines, as in Asti Spumante or Moscato d'Asti. There are several appellations in south-west France for inexpensive Muscats made rather like port, part-fermented before the addition of grape alcohol to halt the conversion of sugar into alcohol, creating a sweet and heady *vin doux naturel*. Dry Muscat wines, when well made, have a delicious sweet aroma but a refreshing, light touch with flavours reminiscent variously of orange blossom, wood smoke and grapefruit.

must – New-pressed grape juice prior to fermentation.

N

Navarra – DO wine-producing region of northern Spain adjacent to, and overshadowed by, Rioja. Navarra's wines can be startlingly akin to their neighbouring rivals, and sometimes rather better value for money.

négociant – In France, a dealer-producer who buys wines from growers and matures and/or blends them for sale under his or her own label. Purists can be a bit sniffy about these entrepreneurs, claiming that only the vine-grower with his or her own winemaking set-up can make truly authentic stuff, but the truth is that many of the best wines of France are *négociant*-produced – especially at the humbler end of the price scale. *Négociants* are often identified on wine labels as *négociant-éleveur* (literally 'dealer-bringer-up'), meaning that the wine has been matured, blended and bottled by the party in question.

Negroamaro – Black grape variety mainly of Puglia, the much-lauded wine region of south-east Italy. Dense, earthy red wines with ageing potential and plenty of alcohol. The grape behind Copertino, Salice Salentio and Squinzano.

Nerello Mascalese – Black grape of Sicily making light, flavoursome and alcoholic reds.

Nero d'Avola – Black grape variety of Sicily and southern Italy. It makes deep-coloured wines that, given half a chance, can develop intensity and richness with age.

non-vintage – A wine is described as such when it has been blended from the harvests of more than one year. A non-vintage wine is not necessarily an inferior one, but under quality-control regulations around the world, still table wines most usually derive solely from one year's grape crop to qualify for appellation status. Champagnes and sparkling wines are mostly blended from several vintages, as are fortified wines, such as basic port and sherry.

nose – In the vocabulary of the wine-taster, the nose is the scent of a wine. Sounds a bit dotty, but it makes a sensible enough alternative to the rather bald 'smell'. The use of the word 'perfume' implies that the wine smells particularly good. 'Aroma' is used specifically to describe a wine that smells as it should, as in 'this burgundy has the authentic strawberry-raspberry aroma of Pinot Noir'.

O

oak – Most of the world's costliest wines are matured in new or nearly new oak barrels, giving additional opulence of flavour. Of late, many cheaper wines have been getting the oak treatment, too, in older, cheaper casks, or simply by having sacks of oak chippings poured into their steel or fibreglass holding tanks. 'Oak aged' on a label is likely to indicate the latter treatments. But the overtly oaked wines of Australia have in some cases been so overdone that there is now a reactive trend whereby some producers proclaim their wines – particularly Chardonnays – as 'unoaked' on the label, thereby asserting that the flavours are more naturally achieved.

Oltrepo Pavese – Wine-producing zone of Piedmont, north-west Italy. The name means 'south of Pavia across the [river] Po' and the wines, both white and red, can be excellent quality and value for money.

organic wine – As in other sectors of the food industry, demand for organically made wine is – or appears to be – growing. As a rule, a wine qualifies as organic if it comes entirely from grapes grown in vineyards cultivated without the use of synthetic materials, and made in a winery where chemical treatments or additives are shunned with similar vigour. In fact, there are plenty of winemakers in the world using organic methods, but who disdain to label their bottles as such. Wines proclaiming their organic status used to carry the same sort of premium as their counterparts round the corner in the fruit, vegetable and meat aisles. But organic viticulture is now commonplace and there seems little price impact. There is no single worldwide (or even Europe-wide) standard for organic food or wine, so you pretty much have to take the producer's word for it.

P

Pasqua – One of the biggest and, it should be said, best wine producers of the Veneto region of north-west Italy.

Passetoutgrains – Bourgogne Passetoutgrains is a generic appellation of the Burgundy region, France. The word loosely means 'any grapes allowed' and is supposed specifically to designate a red wine made with Gamay grapes as well as Burgundy's principal black variety, Pinot Noir, in a ratio of two parts Gamay to one of Pinot. The wine is usually relatively inexpensive, and relatively uninteresting, too.

Pays d'Oc – Shortened form under recent rule changes of French wine designation Vin de Pays d'Oc. All other similar regional designations can be similarly abbreviated.

Pecorino – White grape variety of mid-eastern Italy currently in vogue for well-coloured dry white varietal wines.

Periquita – Black grape variety of southern Portugal. Makes rather exotic spicy reds. Name means 'parrot'.

Perricone – Black grape variety of Sicily. Low-acid red wines.

PET – It's what they call plastic wine bottles – lighter to transport and allegedly as ecological as glass. Polyethylene terephthalate.

Petit Verdot – Black grape variety of Bordeaux used to give additional colour, density and spiciness to Cabernet Sauvignon-dominated blends. Mostly a minority player at home, but in Australia and California it is grown as the principal variety for some big hearty reds of real character.

petrol – When white wines from certain grapes, especially Riesling, are allowed to age in the bottle for longer than a year or two, they can take on a spirity aroma reminiscent of petrol or diesel. In grand mature German wines, this is considered a very good thing.

Picpoul – Grape variety of southern France. Best known in Picpoul de Pinet, a dry white from near Carcassonne in the Languedoc, newly elevated to AOP status. The name Picpoul (also Piquepoul) means 'stings the lips' – referring to the natural high acidity of the juice.

Piemonte – North-western province of Italy, which we call Piedmont, known for the spumante wines of the town of Asti, plus expensive Barbaresco and Barolo and better-value varietal red wines from Barbera and Dolcetto grapes.

Pinotage – South Africa's own black grape variety. Makes red wines ranging from light and juicy to dark, strong and long-lived. It's a cross between Pinot Noir and a grape the South Africans used to call Hermitage (thus the portmanteau name) but turns out to have been Cinsault.

Pinot Blanc – White grape variety principally of Alsace, France. Florally perfumed, exotically fruity dry white wines.

Pinot Grigio – White grape variety of northern Italy. Wines bearing its name are perplexingly fashionable. Good examples have an interesting smoky-pungent aroma and keen, slaking fruit. But most are dull. Originally French, it is at its best in the lushly exotic Pinot Gris wines of Alsace and is also successfully cultivated in Germany and New Zealand.

Pinot Noir – The great black grape of Burgundy, France. It makes all the region's fabulously expensive red wines. Notoriously difficult to grow in warmer climates, it is nevertheless cultivated by countless intrepid winemakers in the New World intent on reproducing the magic appeal of red burgundy. California and New Zealand have come closest, but rarely at prices much below those for the real thing. Some Chilean Pinot Noirs are inexpensive and worth trying.

Pouilly Fuissé – Village and AC of the Mâconnais region of southern Burgundy in France. Dry white wines from Chardonnay grapes. Wines are among the highest rated of the Mâconnais.

Pouilly Fumé – Village and AC of the Loire Valley in France. Dry white wines from Sauvignon Blanc grapes. Similar 'pebbly', 'grassy' or even 'gooseberry' style to neighbouring AC Sancerre. The notion put about by some enthusiasts that Pouilly Fumé is 'smoky' is surely nothing more than word association with the name.

Primitivo – Black grape variety of southern Italy, especially the region of Puglia. Named from Latin *primus* for first, the grape is among the earliest-ripening of all varieties. The wines are typically dense and dark in colour with plenty of alcohol, and have an earthy, spicy style. Often a real bargain.

Priorat – Emerging wine region of Catalonia, Spain. Highly valued red wines from Garnacha and other varieties.

Prosecco – White grape variety of Italy's Veneto region known entirely for the softly sparkling wine it makes. The best come from the DOCG Conegliano-Valdobbiadene, made as spumante ('foaming') wines in pressurised tanks, typically to 11 per cent alcohol and ranging from softly sweet to crisply dry. Now trendy, but the cheap wines – one leading brand comes in a can – are of very variable quality.

Puglia – The region occupying the 'heel' of southern Italy, lately making many good, inexpensive wines from indigenous grape varieties.

Q

QbA – German, standing for Qualitätswein bestimmter Anbaugebiete. It means 'quality wine from designated areas' and implies that the wine is made from grapes with a minimum level of ripeness, but it's by no means a guarantee of exciting quality. Only wines labelled QmP (see next entry) can be depended upon to be special.

QmP – Stands for Qualitätswein mit Prädikat. These are the serious wines of Germany, made without the addition of sugar to 'improve' them. To qualify for QmP status, the grapes must reach a level of ripeness as measured on a sweetness scale – all according to Germany's fiendishly complicated wine-quality regulations. Wines from grapes that reach the stated minimum level of sweetness qualify for the description of Kabinett. The next level up earns the rank of Spätlese, meaning 'late-picked'. Kabinett wines can be expected to be dry and brisk in style, and Spätlese wines a little bit riper and fuller. The next grade up, Auslese, meaning 'selected harvest', indicates a wine made from super-ripe grapes; it will be golden in colour and honeyed in flavour. A generation ago, these wines were as valued, and as expensive, as any of the world's grandest appellations.

Quincy – AC of Loire Valley, France, known for pebbly-dry white wines from Sauvignon grapes. The wines are forever compared to those of nearby and much better-known Sancerre – and Quincy often represents better value for money. Pronounced 'KAN-see'.

Quinta – Portuguese for farm or estate. It precedes the names of many of Portugal's best-known wines. It is pronounced 'KEEN-ta'.

R

racy – Evocative wine-tasting description for wine that thrills the tastebuds with a rush of exciting sensations. Good Rieslings often qualify.

raisiny – Wines from grapes that have been very ripe or overripe at harvest can take on a smell and flavour akin to the concentrated, heat-dried sweetness of raisins. As a minor element in the character of a wine, this can add to the appeal but as a dominant characteristic it is a fault.

rancio – Spanish term harking back to Roman times when wines were commonly stored in jars outside, exposed to the sun, so they oxidised and took on a burnt sort of flavour. Today, *rancio* describes a baked – and by no means unpleasant – flavour in fortified wines, particularly sherry and Madeira.

Reserva – In Portugal and Spain, this has genuine significance. The Portuguese use it for special wines with a higher alcohol level and longer ageing, although the precise periods vary between regions. In Spain, especially in the Navarra and Rioja regions, it means the wine must have had at least a year in oak and two in bottle before release.

reserve – On French (as *réserve*) or other wines, this implies special-quality, longer-aged wines, but has no official significance.

Retsina – The universal white wine of Greece. It has been traditionally made in Attica, the region of Athens, for a very long time, and is said to owe its origins and name to the ancient custom of sealing amphorae (terracotta jars) of the wine with a gum made from pine resin. Some of the flavour of the resin inevitably transmitted itself into the wine, and ancient Greeks acquired a lasting taste for it.

Reuilly – AC of Loire Valley, France, for crisp dry whites from Sauvignon grapes. Pronounced 'RER-yee'.

Ribatejo – Emerging wine region of Portugal. Worth seeking out on labels of red wines in particular, because new winemakers are producing lively stuff from distinctive indigenous grapes such as Castelao and Trincadeira.

Ribera del Duero – Classic wine region of north-west Spain lying along the River Duero (which crosses the border to become Portugal's Douro, forming the valley where port comes from). It is home to an estate rather oddly named Vega Sicilia, where red wines of epic quality are made and sold at equally epic prices. Further down the scale, some very good reds are made, too.

Riesling – The noble grape variety of Germany. It is correctly pronounced 'REEZ-ling', not 'RICE-ling'. Once notorious as the grape behind all those boring 'medium' Liebfraumilches and Niersteiners, this grape has had a bad press. In fact, there has never been much, if any, Riesling in Germany's cheap-and-nasty plonks. But the country's best wines, the so-called Qualitätswein mit Prädikat grades, are made almost exclusively with Riesling. These wines range from crisply fresh and appley styles to extravagantly fruity, honeyed wines from late-harvested grapes. Excellent Riesling wines are also made in Alsace and now in Australia.

Rioja – The principal fine-wine region of Spain, in the country's north east. The pricier wines are noted for their vanilla-pod richness from long ageing in oak casks. Tempranillo and Garnacha grapes make the reds, Viura the whites.

Ripasso – A particular style of Valpolicella wine. New wine is partially refermented in vats that have been used to make the Recioto reds (wines made from semi-dried grapes), thus creating a bigger, smoother version of usually light and pale Valpolicella.

Riserva – In Italy, a wine made only in the best vintages, and allowed longer ageing in cask and bottle.

Rivaner – Alternative name for Germany's Müller-Thurgau grape, the life-blood of Liebfraumilch.

Riverland – Vineyard region to the immediate north of the Barossa Valley of South Australia, extending east into New South Wales.

Roditis – White grape variety of Greece, known for fresh dry whites with decent acidity, often included in retsina.

rosso – Red wine, Italy.

Rosso Conero – DOC red wine made in the environs of Ancona in the Marches, Italy. Made from the Montepulciano grape, the wine can provide excellent value for money.

Ruby Cabernet – Black grape variety of California, created by crossing Cabernet Sauvignon and Carignan. Makes soft and squelchy red wine at home and in South Africa.

Rueda – DO of north-west Spain making first-class refreshing dry whites from the indigenous Verdejo grape, imported Sauvignon, and others. Exciting quality, and prices are keen.

Rully – AC of Chalonnais region of southern Burgundy, France. White wines from Chardonnay and red wines from Pinot Noir grapes. Both can be very good and are substantially cheaper than their more northerly Burgundian neighbours. Pronounced 'ROO-yee'.

S

Saint Emilion – AC of Bordeaux, France. Centred on the romantic hill town of St Emilion, this famous sub-region makes some of the grandest red wines of France, but also some of the best-value ones. Less fashionable than the Médoc region on the opposite (west) bank of the River Gironde that bisects Bordeaux, St Emilion wines are made largely with the Merlot grape, and are relatively quick to mature. The top wines are classified *1er grand cru classé* and are madly expensive, but many more are classified respectively *grand cru classé* and *grand cru*, and these designations can be seen as a fairly trustworthy indicator of quality. There are several 'satellite' St Emilion ACs named after the villages at their centres, notably Lussac St Emilion, Montagne St Emilion and Puisseguin St Emilion. Some excellent wines are made by estates within these ACs, and at relatively affordable prices thanks to the comparatively humble status of their satellite designations.

Salento – Up-and-coming wine region of southern Italy. Many good bargain reds from local grapes including Nero d'Avola and Primitivo.

Sancerre – AC of the Loire Valley, France, renowned for flinty-fresh Sauvignon whites and rarer Pinot Noir reds. These wines are never cheap, and recent tastings make it plain that only the best-made, individual-producer wines are worth the money. Budget brands seem mostly dull.

Sangiovese – The local black grape of Tuscany, Italy. It is the principal variety used for Chianti and is now widely planted in Latin America – often making delicious, Chianti-like wines with characteristic cherryish-but-deeply-ripe fruit and a dry, clean finish. Chianti wines have become (unjustifiably) expensive in recent years and cheaper Italian wines such as those called Sangiovese di Toscana make a consoling substitute.

Saumur – Town and appellation of Loire Valley, France. Characterful minerally red wines from Cabernet Franc grapes, and some whites. The once-popular sparkling wines from Chenin Blanc grapes are now little seen in Britain.

Saumur-Champigny – Separate appellation for red wines from Cabernet Franc grapes of Saumur in the Loire, sometimes very good and lively.

Sauvignon Blanc – French white grape variety now grown worldwide. New Zealand is successfully challenging the long supremacy of French ACs such as Sancerre. The wines are characterised by aromas of gooseberry, fresh-cut grass, even asparagus. Flavours are often described as 'grassy' or 'nettly'.

sec – Dry wine style. French.

secco – Dry wine style. Italian.

Semillon – White grape variety originally of Bordeaux, where it is blended with Sauvignon Blanc to make fresh dry whites and, when harvested very late in the season, the ambrosial sweet whites of Barsac, Sauternes and other appellations. Even in the driest wines, the grape can be recognised from its honeyed, sweet-pineapple, even banana-like aromas. Now widely planted in Australia and Latin America, and frequently blended with Chardonnay to make dry whites, some of them interesting.

sherry – The great aperitif wine of Spain, centred on the Andalusian city of Jerez (from which the name 'sherry' is an English mispronunciation). There is a lot of sherry-style wine in the world, but only the authentic wine from Jerez and the neighbouring producing towns of Puerta de Santa Maria and Sanlucar de Barrameda may label their wines as such. The Spanish drink real sherry – very dry and fresh, pale in colour and served well-chilled – called fino and manzanilla, and darker but naturally dry variations called amontillado, palo cortado and oloroso.

Shiraz – Australian name for the Syrah grape. The variety is the most widely planted of any in Australia, and makes red wines of wildly varying quality, characterised by dense colour, high alcohol, spicy fruit and generous, cushiony texture.

Somontano – Wine region of north-east Spain. Name means 'under the mountains' – in this case the Pyrenees – and the region has had DO status since 1984. Much innovative winemaking here, with New World styles emerging. Some very good buys. A region to watch.

souple – French wine-tasting term that translates into English as 'supple' or even 'docile' as in 'pliable', but I understand it in the vinous context to mean muscular but soft – a wine with tannin as well as soft fruit.

Spätlese – *See* QmP.

spirity – Some wines, mostly from the New World, are made from grapes so ripe at harvest that their high alcohol content can be detected through a mildly burning sensation on the tongue, similar to the effect of sipping a spirit.

spritzy – Describes a wine with a barely detectable sparkle. Some young wines are intended to have this elusive fizziness; in others it is a fault.

spumante – Sparkling wine of Italy. Asti Spumante is the best known, from the town of Asti in the north-west Italian province of Piemonte. The term describes wines that are fully sparkling. Frizzante wines have a less vigorous mousse.

stalky – A useful tasting term to describe red wines with flavours that make you think the stalks from the grape bunches must have been fermented along with the must (juice). Young Bordeaux reds very often have this mild astringency. In moderation it's fine, but if it dominates it probably signifies the wine is at best immature and at worst badly made.

Stellenbosch – Town and region at the heart of South Africa's burgeoning wine industry. It's an hour's drive from Cape Town and the source of much of the country's cheaper wine. Quality is variable, and the name Stellenbosch on a label can't (yet, anyway) be taken as a guarantee of quality.

stony – Wine-tasting term for keenly dry white wines. It's meant to indicate a wine of purity and real quality, with just the right match of fruit and acidity.

structured – Good wines are not one-dimensional, they have layers of flavour and texture. A structured wine has phases of enjoyment: the 'attack', or first impression in the mouth; the middle palate as the wine is held in the mouth; and the lingering aftertaste.

summer fruit – Wine-tasting term intended to convey a smell or taste of soft fruits such as strawberries and raspberries – without having to commit too specifically to which.

superiore – On labels of Italian wines, this is more than an idle boast. Under DOC rules, wines must qualify for the *superiore* designation by reaching one or more specified quality levels, usually a higher alcohol content or an additional period of maturation. Frascati, for example, qualifies for DOC status at 11.5 per cent alcohol, but to be classified *superiore* must have 12 per cent alcohol.

sur lie – Literally, 'on the lees'. It's a term now widely used on the labels of Muscadet wines, signifying that after fermentation has died down, the new wine has been left in the tank over the winter on the lees – the detritus of yeasts and other interesting compounds left over from the turbid fermentation process. The idea is that additional interest is imparted into the flavour of the wine.

Syrah – The noble grape of the Rhône Valley, France. Makes very dark, dense wine characterised by peppery, tarry aromas. Now planted all over southern France and farther afield. In Australia, where it makes wines ranging from disagreeably jam-like plonks to wonderfully rich and silky keeping wines, it is known as Shiraz.

T

table wine – Wine that is unfortified and of an alcoholic strength, for UK tax purposes anyway, of no more than 15 per cent. I use the term to distinguish, for example, between the red table wines of the Douro Valley in Portugal and the region's better-known fortified wine, port.

Tafelwein – Table wine, German. The humblest quality designation, which doesn't usually bode very well.

tank method – Bulk-production process for sparkling wines. Base wine undergoes secondary fermentation in a large, sealed vat rather than in individual closed bottles. Also known as the Charmat method after the name of the inventor of the process.

Tai – White grape variety of north-east Italy, a relative of Sauvignon Blanc. Also known in Italy as Tocai Friulano or, more correctly, Friulano.

Tannat – Black grape of south-west France, notably for wines of Madiran, and lately named as the variety most beneficial to health thanks to its outstanding antioxidant content.

tannin – Well known as the film-forming, teeth-coating component in tea, tannin is a natural compound that occurs in black grape skins and acts as a natural preservative in wine. Its noticeable presence in wine is regarded as a good thing. It gives young everyday reds their dryness, firmness of flavour and backbone. And it helps high-quality reds to retain their lively fruitiness for many years. A grand Bordeaux red when first made, for example, will have purply-sweet, rich fruit and mouth-puckering tannin, but after ten years or so this will have evolved into a delectably fruity, mature wine in which the formerly parching effects of the tannin have receded almost completely, leaving the shade of 'residual tannin' that marks out a great wine approaching maturity.

Tarrango – Black grape variety of Australia.

tarry – On the whole, winemakers don't like critics to say their wines evoke the redolence of road repairs, but I can't help using this term to describe the agreeable, sweet, 'burnt' flavour that is often found at the centre of the fruit in wines from Argentina, Italy and Portugal in particular.

TCA – Dreaded ailment in wine, usually blamed on faulty corks. It stands for 246 *trichloroanisol* and is characterised by a horrible musty smell and flavour in the affected wine. It is largely because of the current plague of TCA that so many wine producers worldwide are now going over to polymer 'corks' and screwcaps.

tears – The colourless alcohol in the wine left clinging to the inside of the glass after the contents have been swirled. Persistent tears (also known as 'legs') indicate a wine of good concentration.

Tempranillo – The great black grape of Spain. Along with Garnacha (Grenache in France) it makes all red Rioja and Navarra wines and, under many pseudonyms, is an important or exclusive contributor to the wines of many other regions of Spain. It is also widely cultivated in South America.

Teroldego – Black grape variety of Trentino, northern Italy. Often known as Teroldego Rotaliano after the Rotaliano region where most of the vineyards lie. Deep-coloured, assertive, green-edged red wines.

tinto – On Spanish labels indicates a deeply coloured red wine. Clarete denotes a paler colour. Also Portuguese.

Toro – Quality wine region east of Zamora, Spain.

Torrontes – White grape variety of Argentina. Makes soft, dry wines often with delicious grapey-spicy aroma, similar in style to the classic dry Muscat wines of Alsace, but at more accessible prices.

Touraine – Region encompassing a swathe of the Loire Valley, France. Non-AC wines may be labelled 'Sauvignon de Touraine' etc.

Touriga Nacional – The most valued black grape variety of the Douro Valley in Portugal, where port is made. The name Touriga now appears on an increasing number of table wines made as sidelines by the port producers. They can be very good, with the same spirity aroma and sleek flavours of port itself, minus the fortification.

Traminer – Grape variety, the same as Gewürztraminer.

Trebbiano – The workhorse white grape of Italy. A productive variety that is easy to cultivate, it seems to be included in just about every ordinary white wine of the entire nation – including Frascati, Orvieto and Soave. It is the same grape as France's Ugni Blanc. There are, however, distinct regional variations of the grape. Trebbiano di Lugana makes a distinctive white in the DOC of the name, sometimes very good, while Trebbiano di Toscana makes a major contribution to the distinctly less interesting dry whites of Chianti country.

Trincadeira Preta – Portuguese black grape variety native to the port-producing vineyards of the Douro Valley (where it goes under the name Tinta Amarella). In southern Portugal, it produces dark and sturdy table wines.

trocken – 'Dry' German wine. It's a recent trend among commercial-scale producers in the Rhine and Mosel to label their wines with this description in the hope of reassuring consumers that the contents do not resemble the dreaded sugar-water Liebfraumilch-type plonks of the bad old days. But the description does have a particular meaning under German wine law, namely that there is only a low level of unfermented sugar lingering in the wine (9 grams per litre, if you need to know), and this can leave the wine tasting rather austere.

U

Ugni Blanc – The most widely cultivated white grape variety of France and the mainstay of many a cheap dry white wine. To date it has been better known as the provider of base wine for distilling into armagnac and cognac, but lately the name has been appearing on wine labels. Technology seems to be improving the performance of the grape. The curious name is pronounced 'OON-yee', and is the same variety as Italy's ubiquitous Trebbiano.

Utiel-Requena – Region and *Denominación de Origen* of Mediterranean Spain inland from Valencia. Principally red wines from Bobal, Garnacha and Tempranillo grapes grown at relatively high altitude, between 600 and 900 metres.

V

Vacqueyras – Village of the southern Rhône Valley of France in the region better known for its generic appellation, the Côtes du Rhône. Vacqueyras can date its winemaking history all the way back to 1414, but has only been producing under its own village AC since 1991. The wines, from Grenache and Syrah grapes, can be wonderfully silky and intense, spicy and long-lived.

Valdepeñas – An island of quality production amidst the ocean of mediocrity that is Spain's La Mancha region – where most of the grapes are grown for distilling into the head-banging brandies of Jerez. Valdepeñas reds are made from a grape they call the Cencibel – which turns out to be a very close relation of the Tempranillo grape that is the mainstay of the fine but expensive red wines of Rioja. Again, like Rioja, Valdepeñas wines are matured in oak casks to give them a vanilla-rich smoothness. Among bargain reds, Valdepeñas is a name to look out for.

Valpolicella – Red wine of Verona, Italy. Good examples have ripe, cherry fruit and a pleasingly dry finish. Unfortunately, there are many bad examples of Valpolicella. Shop with circumspection. Valpolicella Classico wines, from the best vineyards clustered around the town, are more reliable. Those additionally labelled *superiore* have higher alcohol and some bottle age.

vanilla – Ageing wines in oak barrels (or, less picturesquely, adding oak chips to wine in huge concrete vats) imparts a range of characteristics including a smell of vanilla from the ethyl vanilline naturally given off by oak.

varietal – A varietal wine is one named after the grape variety (one or more) from which it is made. Nearly all everyday wines worldwide are now labelled in this way. It is salutary to contemplate that until the present wine boom began in the 1980s, wines described thus were virtually unknown outside Germany and one or two quirky regions of France and Italy.

vegan-friendly – My informal way of noting that a wine is claimed to have been made not only with animal-product-free finings (*see* vegetarian wine) but without any animal-related products whatsoever, such as manure in the vineyards.

vegetal – A tasting note definitely open to interpretation. It suggests a smell or flavour reminiscent less of fruit (apple, pineapple, strawberry and the like) than of something leafy or even root based. Some wines are evocative (to some tastes) of beetroot, cabbage or even unlikelier vegetable flavours – and these characteristics may add materially to the attraction of the wine.

vegetarian wine – Wines labelled 'suitable for vegetarians' have been made without the assistance of animal products for 'fining' – clarifying – before bottling. Gelatine, egg whites, isinglass from fish bladders and casein from milk are among the items shunned, usually in favour of bentonite, an absorbent clay first found at Benton in the US state of Montana.

Verdejo – White grape of the Rueda region in north-west Spain. It can make superbly perfumed crisp dry whites of truly distinctive character and has helped make Rueda one of the best white-wine sources of Europe. No relation to Verdelho.

Verdelho – Portuguese grape variety once mainly used for a medium-dry style of Madeira, also called Verdelho, but now rare. The vine is now prospering in Australia, where it can make well-balanced dry whites with fleeting richness and lemon-lime acidity.

Verdicchio – White grape variety of Italy best known in the DOC zone of Castelli di Jesi in the Adriatic wine region of the Marches. Dry white wines once known for little more than their naff amphora-style bottles but now gaining a reputation for interesting, herbaceous flavours of recognisable character.

Vermentino – White grape variety principally of Italy, especially Sardinia. Makes florally scented soft dry whites.

Vieilles vignes – Old vines. Many French producers like to claim on their labels that the wine within is from vines of notable antiquity. While it's true that vines don't produce useful grapes for the first few years after planting, it is uncertain whether vines of much greater age – say 25 years plus – than others actually make better fruit. There are no regulations governing the use of the term, so it's not a reliable indicator anyway.

Vin de France – In effect, the new Vin de Table of France's morphing wine laws. The term Vin de Table has just about disappeared – or should have, under new legislation introduced in 2010 – and Vin de France installed as the designation of a wine guaranteed to have been produced in France. The label may state the vintage (if all the wine in the blend does come from a single year's harvest) and the grape varieties that constitute the wine. It may not state the region of France from which the wine comes.

vin de liqueur – Sweet style of white wine mostly from the Pyrenean region of south-westernmost France, made by adding a little spirit to the new wine before it has fermented out, halting the fermentation and retaining sugar.

vin de pays – 'Country wine' of France. The French map is divided up into more than 100 vin de pays regions. Wine in bottles labelled as such must be from grapes grown in the nominated zone or *département*. Some vin de pays areas are huge: the Vin de Pays d'Oc (named after the Languedoc region) covers much of the Midi and Provence. Plenty of wines bearing this humble designation are of astoundingly high quality and certainly compete with New World counterparts for interest and value. *See* Indication Géographique Protégée.

vin de table – The humblest official classification of French wine. Neither the region, grape varieties nor vintage need be stated on the label. The wine might not even be French. Don't expect too much from this kind of 'table wine'. *See* Vin de France.

vin doux naturel – Sweet, mildly fortified wine of southern France. A little spirit is added during the winemaking process, halting the fermentation by killing the yeast before it has consumed all the sugars – hence the pronounced sweetness of the wine.

vin gris – Rosé wine from Provence.

Vinho de mesa – 'Table wine' of Portugal.

Vino da tavola – The humblest official classification of Italian wine. Much ordinary plonk bears this designation, but the bizarre quirks of Italy's wine laws dictate that some of that country's finest wines are also classed as mere vino da tavola (table wine). If an expensive Italian wine is labelled as such, it doesn't mean it will be a disappointment.

Vino de mesa – 'Table wine' of Spain. Usually very ordinary.

vintage – The grape harvest. The year displayed on bottle labels is the year of the harvest. Wines bearing no date have been blended from the harvests of two or more years.

Viognier – A grape variety once exclusive to the northern Rhône Valley in France where it makes a very chi-chi wine, Condrieu, usually costing £20 plus. Now, the Viognier is grown more widely, in North and South America as well as elsewhere in France, and occasionally produces soft, marrowy whites that echo the grand style of Condrieu itself. The Viognier is now commonly blended with Shiraz in red winemaking in Australia and South Africa. It does not dilute the colour and is confidently believed by highly experienced winemakers to enhance the quality. Steve Webber, in charge of winemaking at the revered De Bortoli estates in the Yarra Valley region of Victoria, Australia, puts between two and five per cent Viognier in with some of his Shiraz wines. 'I think it's the perfume,' he told me. 'It gives some femininity to the wine.'

Viura – White grape variety of Rioja, Spain. Also widely grown elsewhere in Spain under the name Macabeo. Wines have a blossomy aroma and are dry, but sometimes soft at the expense of acidity.

Vouvray – AC of the Loire Valley, France, known for still and sparkling dry white wines and sweet, still whites from late-harvested grapes. The wines, all from Chenin Blanc grapes, have a unique capacity for unctuous softness combined with lively freshness – an effect best portrayed in the demi-sec (slightly sweet) wines, which can be delicious and keenly priced. Unfashionable, but worth looking out for.

Vranac – Black grape variety of the Balkans known for dense colour and tangy-bitter edge to the flavour. Best enjoyed in situ.

W

weight – In an ideal world the weight of a wine is determined by the ripeness of the grapes from which it has been made. In some cases the weight is determined merely by the quantity of sugar added during the production process. A good, genuine wine described as having weight is one in which there is plenty of alcohol and 'extract' – colour and flavour from the grapes. Wine enthusiasts judge weight by swirling the wine in the glass and then examining the 'legs' or 'tears' left clinging to the inside of the glass after the contents have subsided. Alcohol gives these runlets a dense, glycerine-like condition, and if they cling for a long time, the wine is deemed to have weight – a very good thing in all honestly made wines.

Winzergenossenschaft – One of the many very lengthy and peculiar words regularly found on labels of German wines. This means a winemaking co-operative. Many excellent German wines are made by these associations of growers.

woodsap – A subjective tasting note. Some wines have a fleeting bitterness, which is not a fault, but an interesting balancing factor amidst very ripe flavours. The effect somehow evokes woodsap.

X

Xarel-lo – One of the main grape varieties for cava, the sparkling wine of Spain.

Xinomavro – Black grape variety of Greece. It retains its acidity even in the very hot conditions that prevail in many Greek vineyards, where harvests tend to over-ripen and make cooked-tasting wines. Modern winemaking techniques are capable of making well-balanced wines from Xinomavro.

Y

Yecla – Town and DO wine region of eastern Spain, close to Alicante, making lots of interesting, strong-flavoured red and white wines, often at bargain prices.

yellow – White wines are not white at all, but various shades of yellow – or, more poetically, gold. Some white wines with opulent richness even have a flavour I cannot resist calling yellow – reminiscent of butter.

Z

Zibibbo – Sicilian white grape variety synonymous with north African variety Muscat of Alexandria. Scantily employed in sweet winemaking, and occasionally for drier styles.

Zinfandel – Black grape variety of California. Makes brambly reds, some of which can age very gracefully, and 'blush' whites – actually pink, because a little of the skin colour is allowed to leach into the must. The vine is also planted in Australia and South America. The Primitivo of southern Italy is said to be a related variety, but makes a very different kind of wine.

Index

12-Year-Old Oloroso Sherry, Taste the Difference 108
1531 Blanquette de Limoux, Finest 127
6285 Margaret River Chardonnay 77
6285 Margaret River Merlot 72
Adelaide Hills Chardonnay, M Signature 89
Aglianico del Vulture 75
Aglianico del Vulture Cantina di Venosa 63
AIX Rosé 65
Alba Signature Albariño 44
Albariño Albanta 44
Albariño, M Signature 93
Alsace Gewürztraminer, Finest 123
Alzar Malbec 84
Amarone della Valpolicella Cantine Riondo 37
Amarone, Finest 117
Andara Merlot 26
Anjou Blanc, Tesco 122
Araldica Cortese 68
Araucaria Riesling Pinot Grigio 78
Argentina Torrontes, Finest 120
Argentine Malbec, The Co-operative 46
Argentinean Malbec, Finest 111
Aromatic and Citrus Spanish Dry White, Waitrose 144
Atlantis Santorini 80
Aupouri Sauvignon Blanc 43
Azinhaga de Ouro Douro Reserva 55

Balfour 1503 Brut 70
Barbaresco, Taste the Difference 100
Barbera d'Asti, Extra Special 37
Barbera, The Co-operative 48
Barolo 55
Barolo, Extra Special 37
Barolo, Finest 117
Baron de Ley Rioja Reserva 49
Barossa Shiraz, M Signature 84
Beaujolais 73
Beaujolais, Tesco 113
Beaujolais-Villages Georges Duboeuf 61
Beaujolais Villages, M Signature 85
Beaujolais Villages, Tesco 114
Belmont Pinot Noir 63
Beneventano Aglianico 74
Bianco Terre Siciliane 80
Bienbebido Queso Tempranillo 64
Black Cottage Rosé 66
Blason du Rhône Côtes du Rhône-Villages 132
A Blend of Amontillado Medium Dry Sherry,
  Winemakers' Selection 108
Bodegas Borsao Tres Picos 88
Boekenhoutskloof The Chocolate Block 136
Bolney Estate Autumn Spice 140
Bordeaux Blanc Château Roberperots, Extra
  Special 41
Bordeaux Rosé, Taste the Difference 102
Bordeaux Sauvignon Blanc 90
Bordeaux Supérieur Château Roberperots, Extra
  Special 35
Borgo Molino Motivo Prosecco Brut 128
Bourgogne Chardonnay Les Chenaudières 67
Bourgogne Hautes-Côtes de Beaune 57
Bourgogne Hautes-Côtes de Nuits 57
Brancott Estate Terroir Series Pinot Noir 117
Bushland Estate Shiraz 26
Butcher's Block Bonarda-Malbec 72

Cabernet Sauvignon, Morrisons 87
Caleidoscopio Malbec Touriga Nacional Mourvèdre 72
Californian Cabernet Sauvignon, Waitrose 138
Californian Chardonnay, Waitrose 144
Campo Lindo Organic Sauvignon Blanc, Finest 121
Cantina di Soave 142

Cantina Gadoro Fiano 142
Cape White 81
Casa Luis Cava Rosado 44
Casa Luis Reserva 38
Casal de Ventozela Vinho Verde 68
Cascara Limari Valley Chardonnay 78
Casillero del Diablo Chardonnay 90
Casillero Reserva Privada 34
Castel Boglione Barbera/Cabernet Sauvignon 135
Castillo de Albai Rioja Blanco 106
Castillo de Albai Rioja Tinto 101
Cave de Beblenheim Kleinfels Riesling 141
Cellier des Princes Rosé 89
Cepa Alegro Rioja Reserva, Taste the Difference 101
Cepa Lebrel Rioja Reserva 56
Ch. Fongaban Puisseguin-Saint-Emilion 54
Chablis 57
Chablis Domaine de la Levée, Extra Special 42
Chablis Domaine de Préhy 79
Chablis Domaine Servin 67
Chablis Premier Cru, Finest 124
Chablis Premier Cru, M Signature 91
Chablis, Tesco Finest 123
Champagne Bissinger Brut Rosé 58
Champagne Bissinger Grand Prestige Brut 58
Champagne Blanc de Blancs Brut, Waitrose 145
Champagne Blanc de Blancs Brut, Winemakers'
  Selection 107
Champagne Blanc de Noirs Brut, Winemakers'
  Selection 107
Champagne Brut, M Signature 94
Champagne Rosé Brut, Winemakers' Selection 107
Champagne Veuve Monsigny Brut 29
Chanoine Frères Vintage Champagne 128
Chardonnay, Extra Special 40
Chardonnay Vin de Pays d'Oc 28
Château Cambon La Pelouse 99
Château de La Dauphine 35
Château de Pena Côtes du Roussillon 115
Château Fonguillon Montagne St Emilion 115
Château Fonréaud 48 133
Château Gillet Bordeaux 73
Château Greysac 62
Château Jouanin 47
Château l'Argenteyre 86
Château Laroque 134
Château Liversan 133
Château Roumieu 50
Chateau Saint Jean Chardonnay 69
Château Salmonière Muscadet de Sèvre et Maine
  Sur Lie 41
Château Sénéjac 115
Chateau Tanunda Barossa Cabernet Merlot, Taste
  the Difference 97
Châteauneuf du Pape, Extra Special 36
Châteauneuf du Pape Mont Redon Vignoble
  Abeille 62
Chenin Blanc, Extra Special Fairtrade 43
Chenin Blanc, M Signature 93
Chenin Blanc, Morrisons 93
Chenin Blanc, Simply 126
Chevalier de Fauvert Merlot VdeP 54
Chianti Classico Fortezza dei Colli 55
Chianti Riserva, Extra Special 36
Chianti Riserva, Finest 117
Chilean Pinot Noir, Taste the Difference 97
Chilean Sauvignon Blanc, Extra Special 39
Chorey-lès-Beaune Domaine Maillard Père et Fils 134
Cigales Tempranillo, Wine Atlas 38
Cimaroa Chardonnay 55
Cimarosa Cabernet Sauvignon 55

Cimarosa Malbec Reserva Privada 54
Cimarosa Marlborough Sauvignon Blanc 58
Cimarosa Pedro Jimenez 57
Clare Valley Riesling, The Exquisite Collection 28
Claret Bordeaux AC 54
Claret, Morrisons 85
Claret, Simply 113
Clos St Jacques Gewürztraminer 67
Cloudy Bay Chardonnay 105
Comte de Senneval Champagne Brut 58
Condado de Haza Ribera del Duero Crianza 101
Conde Noble White Wine 58
Cono Sur Bicicleta Pinot Noir 34
Cono Sur Reserva Riesling 90
Corte Mayor Rioja Crianza 49
Côtes Catalanes Grenache, Finest 114
Côtes de Gascogne Blanc, Tesco 122
Côtes de Provence Rosé 56
Côtes de Roussillon, Wine Atlas 35
Côtes de Thau, Wine Atlas 40
Côtes du Rhône Les Fustiers 61
Côtes du Rhône, Morrisons 85
Côtes du Rhône Rosé, Winemakers' Selection 102
Côtes du Rhône Villages, Extra Special 35
Côtes du Rhône Villages Réserve du Boulas Laudun 78
Côtes du Rhône Villages, Taste the Difference 98
Cowrie Bay Sauvignon Blanc 143
Craft 3 Marlborough Sauvignon Blanc 80
Crémant de Limoux Cuvée Royale Brut 145
Crozes Hermitage, Finest 114
Crozes-Hermitage Les Hauts de Pavières 133
Cuartel Merlot, Finest 112
The Cubist Old Vine Garnacha 137
Curicó Valley Chilean Merlot, Taste the Difference 97
Cuvée Fleur Rosé 138

Dão, Extra Special 38
d'Arenberg The Hermit Crab Viognier/ Marsanne 139
Days of Summer 66
De Bortoli Family Reserve Cabernet Sauvignon 33
Denman Semillon, Finest 120
Domaine Chante-Alouette-Cormeil 134
Domaine de la Croix de Chaintres Saumur-
   Champigny 133
Domaine de la Meynarde Plan de Dieu Côtes du
   Rhône Villages 73
Domaine de La Noblaie Chinon, The Co-operative
   Truly Irresistible 48
Domaine de la Pinte Arbois Chardonnay 79
Domaine de l'Estagnol Minervois 54
Domaine de Montval Syrah 61
Domaine de Sours Rosé, Finest 119
Domaine du Colombier Chinon 98
Domaine du Haut-Rauly Monbazillac 50
Domaine Ferrandière Riesling 66
Domaine Paul Blanck Pinot Noir 133
Domaine Sainte Ferréol Viognier 67
Dominio del Plata Terroir Series Malbec 72
Dornfelder 55
Douro, Extra Special 38
Douro, Finest 118
Douro Valley Reserva, Waitrose 136
Dr L Riesling 42
Dr Loosen Graacher Himmelreich Riesling
   Kabinett 104
Dry Manzanilla Superior Sherry, Winemakers'
   Selection 108
The Duke 88

Ebenezer & Seppeltsfield Shiraz 72
El Meson Rioja Gran Reserva, Extra Special 39
Emiliana Organic Viognier 78
Era Costana Rioja Crianza 101
Eric Louis Sancerre Rouge La Côte Blanche 86
Errazuriz Estate Merlot 34
Estevez Cabernet Sauvignon Carmenère Reserva 26
Estevez Carmenère 26

Falua Arinto Reserva 126

Ferngrove Cabernet Sauvignon 46
Ferrari Brut 82
Fetasca Neagra, Wine Atlas 38
Fête du Gris Sauvignon Gris 79
Feteasca Regala, Wine Atlas 43
Fiano, Finest 125
Fiano, M Signature 92
Fief-Guérin Muscadet Sur Lie 140
Filippo Sansovino Millesimato Prosecco Brut
   Magnum 44
Finca Carelio Tempranillo 64
Fino Sherry, Taste the Difference 108
Fisherman's Catch Chenin Blanc 77
Fitou Domaine D'Aubermesnil, Finest 113
Fitou Mme Claude Parmentier 132
Fog Head Reserve Pinot Noir 138
Frapatto, Wine Atlas 36
Freeman's Bay Marlborough Sparkling Wine 30
Freeman's Bay Pinot Gris 28
Freeman's Bay Sauvignon Blanc 28

Gamay Vin de Pays de L'Ardèche 73
Garnacha Rosé, Simply 120
Gavi Broglia, The Co-operative Truly Irresistible 51
Gavi, Finest 125
Gavi, Taste the Difference 105
Gavi, The Exquisite Collection 28
Gigondas Domaine Des Bosquets 116
Gnarly Dudes Shiraz 61
Good Ordinary Claret 132
Graham Beck Antony's Yard 64
Gran Bajoz Toro 38
Grand Conseillier Chardonnay 124
Grand Cru Vintage Champagne Brut, Finest 128
Grand Fief de Retail Muscadet Sèvre et Maine Sur
   Lie 57
Greco di Tufo, Taste the Difference 105
Grenache Rosé, Finest 119
Grillo, Wine Atlas 42
Grüner Veltliner, M Signature 89
Grüner Veltliner, Waitrose 139

H Prinz von Hessen Rheingau Riesling 42
Hen Pecked Picpoul de Pinet 140
Hey Malbec! 61
House Soave, Sainsbury's 104
House Tempranillo, Sainsbury's 100
House White Wine 81
Huntaway Central Otago Pinot Noir 87
Huntaway Reserve Chardonnay 143

I Crinali Nero di Troia 86
Il Venti Rossi 134
Invivo Sauvignon Blanc 68
Italian White 91

Jean Dumont Bourgogne Pinot Noir 54
Jewel of Nasik Sauvignon Blanc 80
Jordan Cabernet Merlot 64
Joseph Drouhin Puligny-Montrachet 1er Cru Les
   Folatières 142
Josmeyer le Fromenteau Pinot Gris 141
Junge Rheingauer Riesling 58

Kalander White 93
Ken Forrester Workhorse Chenin Blanc 81
Kiwi Cove Sauvignon Blanc 43
Koenig Pinot Noir Réserve 54
Koenig Riesling Réserve 57
Kulapelli Cabernet Sauvignon, Finest 112

La Casa Sauvignon Blanc 52
La Côterie Vacqueyras 35
La Folie Douce Pinot Noir 113
La Folie Douce Sauvignon Blanc 122
La Huasa Merlot 73
La Nonna Rioja Crianza 118
La Nonna Rioja Joven 118
La Patrie Côtes de Bordeaux 98
La Posta Bonarda 84
La Sablette Muscadet 90

Lafou El Sender 137
Lambrusco Secco Reggiano 75
Langham Estate Brut Rosé 82
Languedoc Blanc, Taste the Difference 103
Languedoc Rouge, Taste the Difference 99
Las Falleras Tinto 76
Las Lomas Shiraz, Finest 112
Las Moras Pinot Grigio 49
Lateral Pinot Grigio 121
L'Avenir Rosé de Pinotage 102
LaVis Storie di Vite Pinot Grigio 143
Le Cellier Savoyard Apremont 57
Le Grand Ballon Sauvignon Blanc 140
Le Grand Clauzy Sauvignon Blanc 41
Leitz Rüdesheimer Magdalenenkreuz Riesling
    Kabinett 142
Les Caillottes Sancerre Rosé 102
Les Champs Clos Sancerre 99
Les Complices de Loire Les Graviers Chinon 132
Les Crouzes Old Vines Carignan 47
Les Jablières Santenay 55
Les Jamelles Réserve Mourvèdre 47
Les Pionniers Champagne Brut 52
Les Pionniers Vintage Champagne Brut 52
Les Richoises Syrah Rosé 89
Les Voiles de Paulilles Collioure 74
L'Etoile de Begude Chardonnay 67
L'Extra par Langlois Crémant de Loire Brut 70
Leyda Valley Sauvignon Blanc, The Co-operative
    Truly Irresistible 49
LFE Selección de Familia Sauvignon Blanc 40
Libertario La Mancha Red 56
Libra Verdejo, Waitrose 144
Limestone Coast Cabernet Sauvignon, M Signature 84
Limestone Coast Cabernet Sauvignon, The Exquisite
    Collection 26
Lirac Les Closiers 73
Lo Abarca Riesling 79
The Lodge Hill Shiraz 61
Louis Bernard Premier Cru Champagne, Extra
    Special 44
Louis Latour Gevrey-Chambertin 63
Lucien Marcel Vin de Pays du Gers Blanc 122
Luis Felipe Edwards Bin Series Merlot 131
Luisella Bardolino 89
Lussac St-Emilion 54

M de Minuty Rosé 65
Mâcon-Villages Les Chanussots 57
Mâcon Villages, Taste the Difference 103
Mâcon Villages, Tesco 123
Magellan Pinot Noir 62
Malbec, The Co-operative Fairtrade Truly Irresistible 46
Malbec, Winemakers' Selection 97
Malvirà Nebbiolo delle Langhe 135
Maretti Langhe Rosso 63
Marksman Brut Blanc de Blancs 82
Marlborough Sauvignon Blanc, Extra Special 43
Marlborough Sauvignon Blanc, Finest 126
Marlborough Sauvignon Blanc, M Signature 92
Marlborough Sauvignon Blanc, The Exquisite
    Collection 29
Marlborough Sun Pinot Noir 37
Marqués de Cacarés Rioja Gran Reserva 65
Marques De Casa Concha Syrah 84
Marques de Valido Rioja Reserva 48
Marsanne, Wine Atlas 40
Martin Codax Caixas Godello 69
Martinborough Vineyard Te Tera Pinot Noir 64
Marzemino, Wine Atlas 36
Mas du Colombel Faugères 62
Mayu Sangiovese 34
McGuigan The Shortlist Chardonnay 39, 121
Mellow and Fruity Spanish Red, Waitrose 137
Mercurey Béjot 35
Merlot, The Co-operative Fairtrade 46
Meursault, Finest 124

Mezquiriz Navarra Rosé 56
Mineralstein Riesling 80
Miraval Rosé 65
Montelciego Rioja Joven 88
Montepulciano d'Abruzzo 55
Montepulciano d'Abruzzo, M Signature 86
Montepulciano d'Abruzzo, The Co-operative Truly
    Irresistible 48
Montepulciano d'Abruzzo, Winemakers' Selection 99
Montes Reserva Cabernet Sauvignon 46
Montes Reserva Sauvignon Blanc 49
Morador Malbec, Taste the Difference Fairtrade 97
Moulin-à-Vent Château des Jacques 99
Mount Riley Marlborough Sauvignon Blanc 105
Mud House Sauvignon Blanc 143
Muga Rioja Rosado 139
Muriel Rioja Reserva Vendimia Seleccionada 65
Muscadet Sèvre et Maine sur Lie, Taste the
    Difference 103
Muscadet, Simply 121

Natale Verga Primitivo 63
The Ned Pinot Grigio 143
The Ned Pinot Noir 136
Negroamaro 74
Nero d'Avola, Finest 116
Nero d'Avola, M Signature 86
Nero d'Avola Rosé, Finest 119
New Zealand Pinot Noir, Extra Special 37
Nicosia Etna Rosso 75
Norton Winemaker's Reserve Malbec 131
Noster Nobilis Priorat 39

Old Vine Garnacha, Winemakers' Selection 100
Old Vines Garnacha, Extra Special 38
Organic Old Vine Tempranillo 76
Orvieto Classico, The Co-operative 51
Oudinot Brut 82

Palacio de Fefiñanes Albariño 144
Palacio de Vivero Rueda, Extra Special 44
Palataia Pinot Noir 74
Palatia Pinot Grigio 79
Palo Cortado Sherry, M Signature 94
Palo Marcado Old Vines Malbec 111
Pasqua Passimento Bianco 68
Paul Cluver Ferricrete Pinot Noir 76
Paul Mas Clairette 91
Paul Mas Grenache/Syrah Vin de Pays d'Oc 132
Pécharmant Clos Montalbanie 47
Pecorino, Finest 126
Pecorino Umani Ronchi 80
Peter & Peter Riesling Mosel 125
Peter Yealands Sauvignon Blanc 51
Petit Chablis, M Signature 91
Petit Chablis, Taste the Difference 104
Philippe Michel Crémant de Jura 29
Pichi Richi Chardonnay 77
Pichi Richi Shiraz 72
Pierre-Jean Sauvion Chenin Blanc 66
Pietrariccia Fiano 68
Pinot Grigio, Extra Special 43
Pinot Gris, M Signature 90
Pinot Noir, The Co-operative Truly Irresistible 47
Pinot Noir, The Interlude 46
Pinot Noir Vignobles Rousselet 27
Pinotage, Morrisons 87
Pinotage, Simply 118
Pisano Cisplatino Tannat 77
Piwen Chardonnay, Finest 121
Porta 6: 64
Portuguese Red, Winemakers' Selection 100
Portuguese Rosé, Simply 119
Pouilly-Fumé Jonathan Pabiot 67
Pouilly Fumé, Taste the Difference 104
Premier Cru Champagne Brut, Finest 127
Première Anjou Chenin Blanc 50
Première Vouvray 91
Primitivo, Extra Special 36

Prosecco Valdobbiadene Superiore Extra Dry 29
Prosecco, Waitrose 145
Provence Rosé, Waitrose 138
Quinta de Azeveda Vinho Verde 144
Rachel's Chenin Blanc 69
Raso de la Cruz Blanco 82
Raso de la Cruz Tinto 76
Red Burgundy, M Signature 85
Red on Black 74
Reichsgraf von Kesselstatt Riesling Kabinett 50
Renato Ratti Langhe Nebbiolo 76
Reserva Carmenère, Waitrose 131
Reuilly Cuvée Prestige Fiefs des Comelias 57
Rheinhessen Dornfelder Rosé, Winemakers'
  Selection 102
Ribera del Duero Altos de Tamaron 56
Ribera del Duero Bodegas Buena Allende La Vega 137
Rickshaw Chardonnay 69
Riesling Feinherb Mosel 58
Riesling, Simply 124
Riesling, Winemakers' Selection 104
Ripasso di Valpolicella Classico Superiore, Waitrose 135
Ripe and Juicy Spanish Rosé, Waitrose 138
Rocca Murer Sauvignon Blanc 143
Romanian Pinot Noir, Waitrose 136
Rully Domaine Marguerite Dupasquier 42
Saint-Aubin 1er Cru Gérard Thomas et Filles 68
Saint Clair James Sinclair Sauvignon Blanc 81
Saint-Véran Vignerons des Grandes Vignes 140
Sancerre La Franchotte, Waitrose 141
Sancerre Rosé, Finest 119
Sancerre, Taste the Difference 104
Sangiovese Superiore, M Signature 86
Sauternes Château Mauras 58
Sauternes, Waitrose 142
Sauvignon Blanc, Morrisons 93
Sauvignon Colombard, Winemakers' Selection 103
Savoie Blanc Coeur Terroir 79
Selaks Reserve Merlot Cabernet 63
Serabel Côtes du Rhône Villages Chusclan 54
Shiraz, Extra Special 34
Sicilian Red, Tesco 116
The Siren Fairtrade Chenin Chardonnay Viognier 51
Sister's Run Barossa Grenache 111
SO Organic Shiraz Vin de Pays d'Oc 98
South African Shiraz Cabernet, Winemakers'
  Selection 100
South African Shiraz, M Signature 88
Springfield Estate Special Cuvée Sauvignon Blanc 144
Squinzano Orbitali Riserva 37
St Chinian, Finest 114
St Emilion Grand Cru 55
St Hallett Old Block Shiraz 111
St Joseph Cuvée D'Automne 115
St Véran Domaine des Valanges 50
Steillage Riesling, Finest 124
Stellenbosch Drive Chardonnay 51
Stellenbosch Drive Fairtrade Shiraz 48
Stellenrust Pinotage 76
Surprisingly Good Pinot Noir 87
Swartland Chenin Blanc, Finest 127
Swartland Pinotage, Finest 118
Taittinger Comtes de Champagne Blanc de Blancs
  Brut 145
Tapada de Villar Vinho Verde 81
Teroldego, Finest 116
Terra Rossa Cabernet Sauvignon Parker Estate 111
Terre da Vino Barolo Riserva 135
Terrunyo Carmenere 112
Thelema Sutherland Chardonnay 51
Tierra Y Hombre Sauvignon Blanc 78

Tilimuqui Single Vineyard Fairtrade Organic
  Cabernet Sauvignon/Bonarda 131
Tilimuqui Single Vineyard Fairtrade Organic
  Torrontes 139
Tim Adams Clare Valley Riesling 120
Tim Adams Clare Valley Semillon 120
Tinto da Anfora 136
Toro Loco Rosé 27
Toro Loco Tempranillo 27
Torre del Falco Nero di Troia 135
Torrontes, M Signature 89
Toscana Rosso 74
Touraine Sauvignon Blanc Domaine Jacky Marteau 78
Touraine Sauvignon Blanc, M Signature 90
Touraine Sauvignon Blanc, Wine Atlas 41
Trésor de Loire Cuvée 845 Chenin Blanc 103
Trivento Reserve Malbec 33
Tsantali Organic Cabernet Sauvignon 134
Uco Valley Malbec, The Exquisite Collection 26
Underwood Pinot Noir 77
Vacqueyras Les Hauts de la Ponche 62
Valdivieso Single Vineyard Cabernet Franc 85
Valpolicella Cantina di Soave 135
Valpolicella Ripasso 75
Valpolicella, Tesco 116
Valpolicella Valpantena 75
Verdicchio Classico dei Castelli di Jesi, Taste the
  Difference 105
Verdicchio, M Signature 92
Vibrant and Grassy Chilean White, Waitrose 139
Vignale Pinot Grigio Rosé Blush 138
Vignobles Roussellet Sauvignon Blanc 28
Villemarin Picpoul de Pinet 66
Vin de Pays d'Oc Merlot, Winemakers' Selection 98
Vin de Pays Gascogne Gros Manseng Sauvignon
  Blanc, Finest 123
Viña Lorea Rioja Crianza, Waitrose 137
Viña Mara Rioja Reserva, Finest 119
Viña Mayu Dry Pedro Ximenez 66
Viña Pomal Blanco 127
Viñalba Reservado de la Familia Malbec 84
Viñedos Barrihuelo Rioja Blanco, Taste the
  Difference 106
Vineyards Merlot 112
Vinho Verde, Morrisons 92
Vinho Verde, Tesco 126
Vinho Verde, Winemakers' Selection 106
Vintage Claret, Tesco 113
Vinya Carles Priorat Crianza 56
Viognier, Extra Special 40
Viognier Pays d'Oc, The Co-operative Truly
  Irresistible 40
Vouvray Château de Montfort 141
Vouvray, Tesco 122
Waikato River Pinot Noir 87
Waikato River Sauvignon Blanc 92
Waimea Estate Pinot Gris 68
Wairarapa Pinot Noir, The Exquisite Collection 27
The Wanted Zin 87
White Burgundy, Extra Special 41
White Burgundy, Tesco 123
White Burgundy, Waitrose 140
White Douro, M Signature 92
Yalumba Y Series Pinot Grigio 49
Yalumba Y Series Viognier 103
Yarra Valley Pinot Noir, Extra Special 33
Zalze Reserve Chenin Blanc 106
Zilzie Merlot 33
Zilzie Shiraz Viognier 33